Simple Composition

Charles Wuorinen

C. F. PETERS CORPORATION
NEW YORK · LONDON · FRANKFURT

SIMPLE COMPOSITION

C. F. Peters Corporation
373 Park Avenue South
New York, NY 10016

PRINTED IN THE UNITED STATES OF AMERICA

Library of Congress Cataloging-in-Publication Data

Wuorinen, Charles.
Simple composition/Charles Wuorinen
p. cm.
Originally published: New York: Longman, c1979.
Includes bibliographical references (p.) and index.
ISBN 0-938856-06-5
1. Composition (Music) 2. Twelve-tone system. I. Title.
MT40.W9 1994
781.3' 1268--dc20 94-27513
CIP
MN

Cover design: Hank Haffner

Contents

PART 4 Form

Preface

A book about composition cannot help being "theoretical." We are talking about potential rather than actual compositions, and our discourse necessarily involves a healthy bit of abstraction. But in our age, standards of discourse about music are so diffuse that before setting out, we must give some thought to what we mean by "theory," and try to show how it relates to our efforts here.

In science, observations of phenomena are made and generalized inferences are drawn from the observations. A theory then emerges, which has the power to predict future events. In this sense, theory precedes practice. But in science, the theory can be tested by external criteria; if it doesn't predict correctly, it is discarded.

In art also, theory usually arises from observation—but on art works themselves, determining those which have worth and meaning is often a highly subjective enterprise. Theory here is a generalization from existing art works, which, however, are neither validated nor invalidated by the theory. In other words, artistic theory has only a limited predictive role.

What is the relation between theory and practice in composition? Theory is usually analytic—that is, it purports to describe and "explain" existing works; and sometimes it is prescriptive—that is, it presumes to tell us how pieces not yet composed ought to be written. However, most of this activity is carried out by non-composers, and is addressed to other non-composers. Thus, while much of what they offer is interesting and valuable, it is of only limited use to composers themselves. On the other hand, this book is written by a composer and is addressed to other composers—intending or actual, amateur or professional. Thus it is similar in intent to certain older books on the subject (like Morley*, for instance). It outlines present practice, and while it can be used for purely didactic purposes, it can also be employed in composing "real" music.

Indeed, most books of musical instruction used to be like this. They presented a rationalized, reasonably rigorous model of real life. What they contained could therefore be used by students in their later professional practice. Unfortunately, this is not true today. What is normally called "theory" usually deals with certain calisthenic routines (tonal harmony and counterpoint) involving music of the past—music of a type no longer composed. We find ourselves at the end of a long conservative trend in theoretical works, a trend which began in the seventeenth century and has accelerated into our own time, with the result that very little is available for the student who wishes some contact with present practice.

*Morley, Thomas, *A Plaine and Easie Introduction to Practical Musicke* (1597), reprinted, Ridgewood, New Jersey: Gregg Press, 1970.

None of the foregoing need deny the value of calisthenic theory. It teaches discipline, and at its best it not only offers insights into the music from which it has been abstracted, but also teaches the fundamental lesson of art—that limitations must exist for free and fruitful artistic creation. For our subject, however, we must depart from the calisthenic tradition. Also, we must recognize that although there seems to be a tendency toward a unification and synthesis of compositional approaches in these years, there is as yet no generally accepted common practice for composition. This last consideration, as well as the very nature of our subject, necessitates a more personal approach than we might adopt for a book dealing with another field.

This book outlines compositional procedures and devices. It tries to tell *how*, and presumes to touch only a little on *why*. Thus, while it is often general and abstract, it is nevertheless a practical manual. In particular, it is not analytic—that sphere we leave to our scholarly colleagues.

This book is based on personal experience; it is a practical, not a speculative or encyclopedic work. Moreover, it does not disguise evaluative attitudes. A scholar may need to do so in the name of objectivity, but an artist cannot. A composer must have such attitudes in order to function at all—such attitudes are a practical professional prerequisite. Therefore, they are openly expressed in this book—in part because it cannot be otherwise, and in part because they may serve as an example of what the user must develop in himself in order to compose. Let him develop his own evaluative attitudes, and let them be different from those expressed here! Each composer asserts what music is through his works; and when he speaks of the nature of music, it is from his direct experience of making it. So it is with all the judgments made in this book.

ACKNOWLEDGMENTS

Much of this book deals with the 12-tone system. All who have concerned themselves with this musical system know the indispensable seminal contributions of Milton Babbitt, whose profound thought in and about music has done so much to shape the 12-tone universe. Without his original efforts, few of the ideas in this book could have taken shape.

It is also my pleasure to acknowledge the influence of Benjamin Boretz, in his writings and in conversation, on my own ideas about music.

Finally, I am grateful for the kindness and thoroughness of my editor, Gerald Warfield.

I am grateful to C. F. Peters, publisher of my music for twenty-five years, for reissuing SIMPLE COMPOSITION after a brief period out of print. In writing this book, I intended it primarily as a guide for composers in search of practical advice and models of how one might work compositionally. But since my presentation made extensive use of the twelve-tone system in its simplest and most easily describable from, the book was taken as a primer in that system. The fact that I used twelve-tone relations for convenience and only because of their simplicity was somehow overlooked.

Perhaps today in 1994 the book may make a slightly different contribution than it did originally: to offer a basic outline of a musical system and method that has proved immensely rich since its introduction by Schoenberg seventy-five years ago, as well as to provide a few practical tips.

--Charles Wuorinen

PART I

The Basic Nature of The 12-Tone System

These different representations of the same C major triad all mean the same thing, functionally—they all, for instance, denote a tonic chord in C major. Even though the registral order (from low to high) in which the constituent tones are presented is different in each case, the role played by each tone is the same. Of course, on a level of greater detail, we recognize individual differences among them, but from a general tonal point of view, they are equivalent. How can this be so? It is possible here because we are dealing with only three tones. Because there are so few, we have no trouble recognizing them—and the intervals between them—by their mere presence alone; in other words, we recognize pitch and interval *content*. At this fundamental level we do not need to impose any other supporting criteria, such as *order* of presentation of pitches to help in recognition.

We see, then, that for the most fundamental relationships of the tonal system—those involving basic harmonic succession, as well as modulation—the moving force is *content recognition*. Now naturally, perceiving themes, and other matters of greater detail, requires the recognition of patterns of order—but for the most fundamental triadic chord-successional unfoldings, all we need is the ability to tell which tones are present.

With 4-tone chords, it already becomes somewhat more difficult to achieve such recognition; we can still do it, but we are helped by the fact that these are usually "seventh" chords, which include the three familiar triadic tones and their intervals as well as the interval of the seventh. As the tonal system evolved toward greater complexity during the nineteenth century, more and more such constructs entered the pitch-relational arena, and they tended, moreover, to be less and less closely related to their triadic originators: Diminished sevenths, augmented chords and the like are really symmetric divisions of the octave into parts of equal size, and therefore remain invariant (in respect to interval content) when inverted. Thus, for instance, when a diminished seventh chord is run through its four possible inversions, it still always contains, basically, only three minor thirds. From this we begin to see that by this stage, pitch and interval content will no longer be a sufficient basic criterion for pitch-relational coherence. As more and more tones out of an available total of twelve come to be present in the texture of tonal music, a unique interval content for chords and melodic lines becomes harder and harder to recognize. Consider, for example, a 13th chord:

EXAMPLE 2

If this sonority occurs in C major, it states the entire collection of tones that make up the scale of that key. It is therefore a far less persuasive generator of a sense of harmonic progress than are the simpler triadic formations; triads contain only three of the available scale tones of the key they inhabit, and can thus be succeeded by other triads in the same key that add new pitches to the ones already present in the texture. As the tonal system evolved, chords like example 2, and indeed even the more frequent seventh chords, were seen increasingly to be the result of contrapuntal detail and elision—and furthermore, chromatic tones foreign to the basic key began to occur with greater and greater frequency. Indeed, by mid-nineteenth century, the radical music of Wagner had become so contrapuntally chromatic that it is hard to assign much of it clearly to any specific key, even though its constituent sonorities are still triadic in origin. In other words, more and more distinct members of the chromatic octave came to unroll in each given time span—both because of the addition of new tones to triadic sonorities and because of the increasing frequency of highly chromatic contrapuntal motion. Thus, for instance, to take a relatively trivial example, a diatonic auxilliary tone is replaced by a chromatically altered tone:

EXAMPLE 3

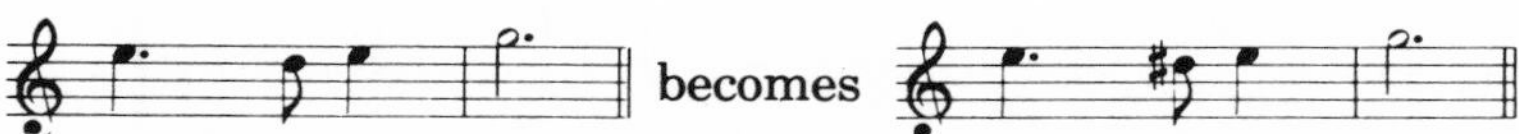

Taken from this standpoint, we can regard the 12-tone system as the result of the tendency within tonal music for an ever increasing number of foreign, ancillary tones to be introduced into the harmonic fabric. In the 12-tone system, all the available twelve tones are, in principal at least, present all the time, in free circulation. Obviously here, pitch *content* cannot have a fundamental organizational meaning (however significant it may be in matters of local detail). Something else is needed. It is found in the imposition of patterns of *order* on the total pitch vocabulary: order of pitch and interval occurrence, expressed not as a surface specific, but as a fundamental structural principle.

This, then, is the main difference between the tonal and the 12-tone systems: The tonal system is based upon interval *content*, the 12-tone system upon interval *order*.

But this difference should not distract us from the many similarities: The two systems make use of the same basic materials—tones and intervals within the same equal-tempered tuning system. Moreover, the long evolution of the tonal system during the nineteenth century, as well as the composition of "freely" chromatic music by Schoenberg and his school (*before* the explicit formulation of the 12-tone system at the beginning of the second quarter of the present century) suggest that the two systems are not dichotomous and disjunct, but parts of a larger whole—however well defined their domains within that whole may be.

The 12-Tone System Introduced

A melody containing all twelve tones and returning to the starting tone can be translated into a more abstract and general form by eliminating everything in the re-expression except the *order* of tones, and the tones themselves, without regard to their registral positions.

EXAMPLE 4-a

Freed from specifics of octave position, articulation, and the like, this series of tones can now be reinterpreted and re-expressed in an infinity of ways, some of them quite distant from the original motive.

EXAMPLE 4-b

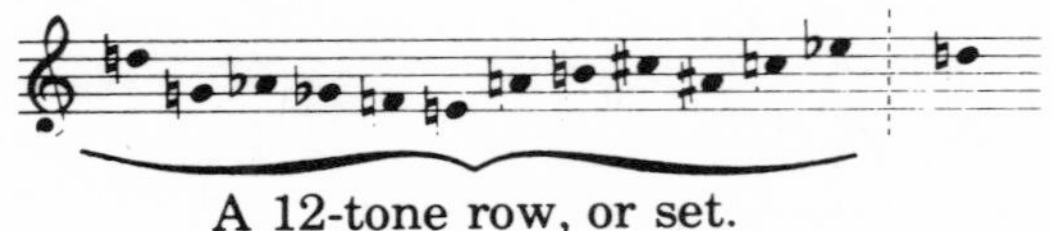

A 12-tone row, or set.

Example 4-b, containing each of the twelve tones once and only once, is an example of a 12-tone row, or *set*. Example 4-a, showing a musically concrete expression of this 12-tone set, also gives a clue to how such an abstract ordering was originally arrived at by Schoenberg.

Twelve-tone sets originally grew out of motives. That is, motives and *thematic* entities became progressively more abstracted until Schoenberg conceived the idea of an abstract source for all the material, melodic and harmonic, in a given work: the twelve tones (or, as we shall see later, more correctly, the twelve pitch classes) in a single unique *ordering*. For this reason, 12-tone sets originally appeared as fundamentally thematic constructs, and other aspects such as verticalization (the stating of several adjacent elements of a set as a chord or simultaneity) were only corollaries. This original sense of what these constructs are has tended to persist even into the present, although we now have a much more general idea of what they can be made to do in composition. So, the original state of affairs within the 12-tone system is one that views 12-tone sets as abstracted theme-sources, and therefore as entities functioning most naturally on a local scale, producing actual melodic and harmonic successions and combinations: the note-to-note continuity of pieces—and only incidentally having larger organizing powers over broader spans of the pieces in which they are employed.

But later, particularly after the Second World War, the notion of what a 12-tone set can do becomes quite generalized: sets become more global in their organizing power, more abstracted and general, and broader in the domain of their compositional influence. This comes about not merely by their being "extended" into regions of compositional activity other than the choice of pitch, but more fundamentally by a change in the notion of the range over which they can be made to function compositionally. In other words, as we shall see in due course, 12-tone sets today have been given the capacity to span larger and larger areas of pieces, and to control the large-scale unfolding of the music they generate as well as the local detail.

To take a small-scale example, the 12-tone set of example 4-b could be expanded so that new tones are nested "inside" the main original tones of the set.

EXAMPLE 4-c

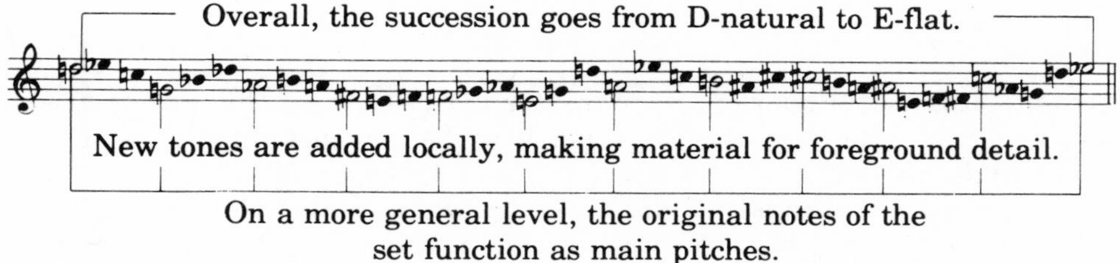

The new tones in example 4-c come from inserting 2-tone groups, which are segments of the main original set in retrograde, twice through; and adding two 3-tone groups at the end, so that the cycle is complete when the line arrives at the last E-flat. In this way, the set is made to function in two different time scales. Now, we could make example 4-c musically concrete in the following, rather trivial, way—one that would express literally the main/subsidiary pitch hierarchy. In the following realization, the main tones are on the beat:

EXAMPLE 4-d

Notice the wide registral spread in this working out, and the tendency to keep duplicated pitches nearby in the same octave position.

If we want to be a bit more subtle, and avoid so periodic an expression, we might do something like the following, which has no special articulative stress on the main tones:

EXAMPLE 4-e

Actually, it is not the aperiodicity of rhythm in this example that avoids stressing the tones of the original set; rather it is the fact that these tones do not have privileged accentual positions—as, for instance, on strong beats.

These examples encapsulate the tendency we have been discussing: to regard 12-tone sets as generators of more than merely local pitch successions. Is there an even more general view of what they are? Perhaps so. Today we tend to consider the fundamental characteristic of 12-tone sets, and the twelve-tone system as a whole, as *interval order*—that is, that ordered successions of intervals are the main determinants of musical coherence. In this view, even twelve-ness, and the non-repetition of pitches before the entire collection of twelve has been exhausted, cease to have the fundamental significance they were once thought to possess.

Here are two pitch successions, which are transpositions of each other:

EXAMPLE 5

(a)

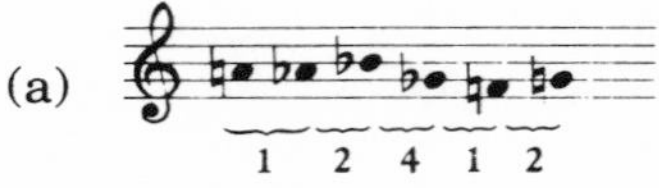

transposed by three semitones becomes:

(b)

These numbers define in semitones the intervals between adjacent tones.

This succession of intervals is the same as that of (a).

Even though the specific tones are different in the two representations, the interval succession is identical. The fact that we recognize these two successions, in a sense, as the *same* succession implies that the real organizing force here is not in the tones, but in the intervals. Indeed, the only thing that makes us able to regard the second succession as a transposition of the first is this very identity of interval succession.

If the principle of ordered interval succession becomes a sufficiently generalized generator of form, then (as is already the case in some 12-tone music) the principles of pitch organization derived from interval content (that we discussed above with respect to chord recognition) can be reintroduced into what is basically order-determined music. This appears to be the direction of highly chromatic music of the present day, and perhaps in the future we shall hear a reconciliation of the two principles of pitch organization, content and order—or rather their unification in a superior whole. This, if it occurs, will serve to demonstrate our assertion that the tonal and 12-tone systems are not really separate musical entities.

Certainly, for example, one may regard small segments of 12-tone sets (such as 3-tone groups) as content groups rather than as rigidly ordered—this does not affect the overall succession defined by the set, but does allow for flexibility in detail. Here, then, is a 12-tone set in which successive 3-tone groups are regarded individually as unordered, or order-free, while the overall succession of the four 3-tone groups *is* ordered:

EXAMPLE 6-a

A strictly ordered succession:

becomes:

from which the tones of each group may be internally re-ordered at pleasure, for instance as:

Before proceeding to our first exercises, a remark should be made on the spelling of pitches in a world without the *a priori* functional relations of the tonal system, in which the twelve tones are in constant circulation. Two principles should be observed:

1. Place an accidental before *every* note head, in the manner of the examples. This removes all possible ambiguity about whether a note is sharp, flat, or natural; and the visual consistency the practice produces more than makes up for the slight extra labor in writing. Moreover, this method is preferred by most performers. (It should be noted that there are contending views on this subject, but our suggestion here is based on practical, not theoretical, experience.)

Now even these larger constructs (the "diatonic" and "chromatic") must be thought of as parts of a more generous whole. That whole is the domain of music based on pitch.

Actually, when we assert pitch as the absolute primary element in music, we are only following universal tradition. But in the past century, the domain claimed by music for its proper exercise, and therefore the materials it feels able to employ, have been so much enlarged that we must likewise present a broadened definition of pitch to sustain our assertion of its primacy. Therefore, we want to include under the rubric of "pitch" not only tones in the usual sense, but noises too—on the ground that they are, in their musical employment, merely sounds less precisely located than pitches within the frequency range that human ears can comprehend. In this definition, then, there is not a dichotomy between "pitch" and "noise," but rather a continuum between more exact and less exact pitch.

A flute playing  concentrates most of its acoustical energy on the fundamental frequency of the written pitch. A bassoon playing  has less energy on the fundamental, but there is still no doubt about what pitch is sounding. A viola playing  *ponticello* (near the bridge) may cause the written pitch almost to disappear in a welter of upper partials—which are, however, still harmonically related to the fundamental. A chime playing  may create some doubt about the octave in which the tone is sounding; furthermore, it possesses inharmonic partials. A bell playing the same tone is even less well defined. A triangle, though "clear" in sound, almost obscures the sense of pitch. A cymbal pitched in the same range as this tone is a band of complex, shifting, inharmonic partials. And a band of electronically produced white noise obscures all sense of pitch whatever (unless it is a very narrow band). In addition to all this, the context in which a sound occurs will greatly affect our sense of the exactness of its pitch.

All of the foregoing should serve to demonstrate that there is, for musical purposes, a rather smooth continuity between the poles of exact pitch and undifferentiated noise; that the division between pitch and noise is contextual and to some extent arbitrary. Nevertheless, a basic cleavage has always existed in music between *tones* and the other sounds music may employ. Whether this results from blind convention or something else need not concern us here, but we must point out a fundamental difference between the organization of pitches and the organization of other sounds in music. Pitches form a stepped continuum (in the West, uniform semitones) which is divided into larger, equal recurring intervals (octaves); in other words, pitches are *modularly* arranged, and we shall see that this has powerful implications. In

EXAMPLE 11

This interval 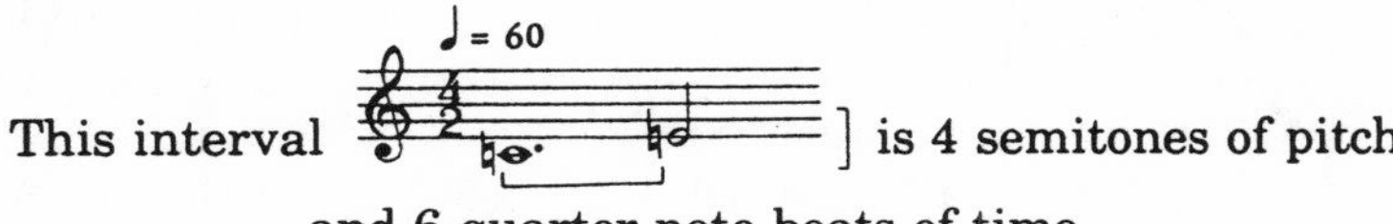

] is 4 semitones of pitch

and 6 quarter-note beats of time

Returning now to our main argument, we can observe that the successful operation of a content-based pitch system demands first of all that its content groups be recognizable. The content group, to be identified, must have a small enough number of elements to allow for quick apperception. And of course, the number of elements must be substantially smaller than the total available pitch vocabulary, so that the distinction between it and the rest of the tones available within the system can be immediately grasped. In tonal music, the triad fulfills these requirements because a 3-tone group has so few elements, and therefore contains so few intervals. Its success as the basic referential content-group in the tonal system is largely due to the fact that its tones can be rearranged, or permuted, in so many ways—especially (in pitch terms) by inversions and (in time terms) by arpeggiations—while still preserving the basically recognizable interval content. The triad also possesses many special characteristics that fit it for its role in tonal music. Without going into burdensome detail, one may observe that the triad is the only sonority within the framework of diatonic functionally-defined consonance and dissonance that has a consonant interval between every pair of tones. (An alternate way of stating this characteristic is to say that the triad defines those intervals of tonal music that are consonant—i.e., it contains *all* the consonant intervals.)

The triad is a 3-tone selection out of a total available vocabulary of twelve. Furthermore, there are pre-defined distances and relationships among the various triads built on the scale steps of any given key. An entire key, with all its internal hierarchy of relationships, makes use of only seven of the total twelve pitches available for tonal music. Let us summarize these relations of inequality in the following example:

EXAMPLE 12

In C major: The *tonic* is the most important tone of the *tonic triad*

which is the most important collection of the *C-major scale collection*

which is the most important collection of the *total chromatic*

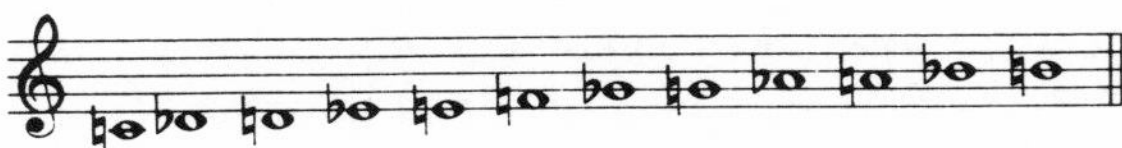

which is the total of all available tones in the tonal system.

The diatonic collection of a tonal piece is always present as a structural "backdrop." Notes outside of this collection are dependent on the notes to which they resolve *or* they imply a new diatonic collection. In 12-tone music, on the other hand, the total pitch vocabulary is always present—in principle if not in actuality. This means that the total of twelve tones can always be called upon at any moment, unlike the case with tonal music, in which non-key-related tones have only an incidental importance. Thus, we have a situtation that is trivial from the point of view of organization by pitch content: The content is always the same, always the totality. Some other organizing force is needed, and this force is found by *ordering* the occurrence of the twelve tones in some consistent way. That is why 12-tone music is based on ordered successions of pitches and intervals. It is this unique status that such an ordered succession (usually a 12-tone set) has in a specific work that provides the organizing power of the 12-tone system. Later, we shall see that although the use of ordered successions arose historically as a means of rendering coherent an homogenous chromatic continuum, the importance of ordered successions is what really determines the force of the system; the number of elements being ordered (twelve, in the usual case) is less significant. Indeed we seem today to be moving into an expanded sense of the 12-tone system in which twelveness is becoming relatively unimportant.

The following example may be contrasted with example 12:

EXAMPLE 13

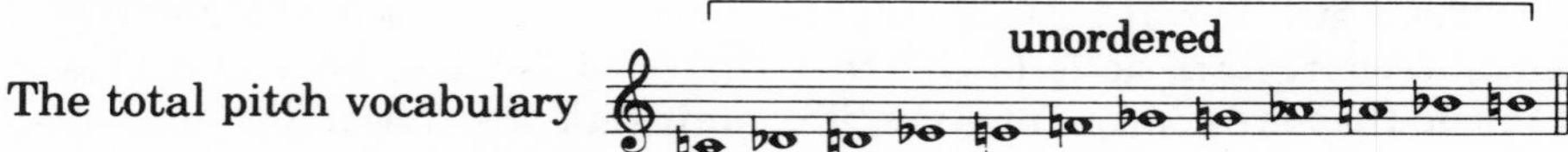

has order characteristics imposed on it, such as

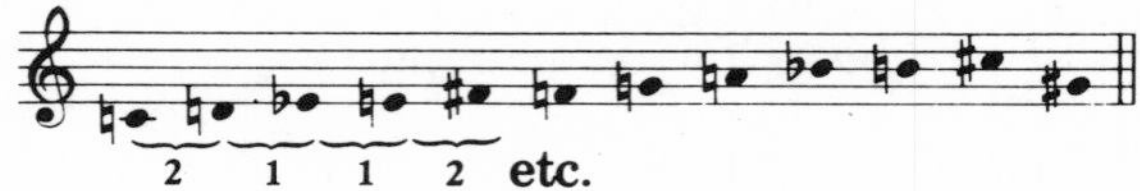

which can be used to control the relations among the 12 tones.

Much has been made of the gulf between the tonal and the 12-tone systems, and the different principles that guide them. Are these two principles, content and order, exclusive? Perhaps not so much as may first appear. For example, a piece might be organized in terms of content on one level of generality, and in terms of order on another. Thus in tonal music, the most fundamental producer of coherence in a given key is the content principle of tonality: You can't have G major without the tones of its scale, and at least some of the relations among triads produced by the degree and kind of their pitch-intersection and embodied in chord successions within the key. But if the music has tunes (and we hope it does), they will constitute ordered successions of tones and durations; usually they will be transformed only very simply (by transposition to another key, for instance). Their very existence and functioning as themes depends on their note-and-duration order being held virtually unchanged throughout their several reappearances. This is shown in example 14:

EXAMPLE 14

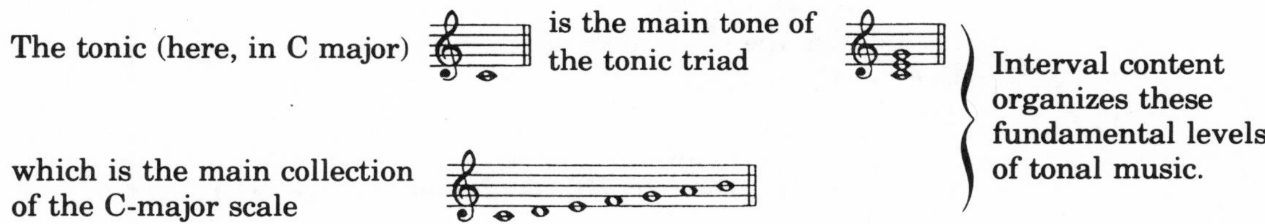

which is a theme for some piece.

On the thematic level, as demonstrated in the last stage of example 14, interval order (of pitch and time) takes over from content principles as the organizing force.

Complimentarily, in 12-tone music, while an interval succession such as a 12-tone set governs the basic structure of the work (the intervallic environment, perhaps the large-scale unfolding, etc.), certain successions of notes may be more significant as content groups than as representatives of the more basic interval succession:

EXAMPLE 15

and a tune made from these content groups, preserving only the order of the 3-tone groups, not the internal ordering of each group's tones:

Here, interval order organizes on a fundamental level, because the *order* of elements in the set (generated as the second stage of the example) determines the *content* of the 3-note groups in the third stage; and unordered interval content organizes on the surface level.

EXERCISES

1. Using the 3-note divisions given in example 15, write a line consisting of several repetitions of these content-groups, as in the example. Choose registers freely.
2. Now divide the set into three unordered 4-note groups. Compose a line in the same way.
3. Transpose this last line twice, once by 6 semitones (the interval between the first pitch of the set and the first pitch of the second 4-note group), then by 10 semitones. Compare the several expressions of the set.

Definitions

We come now to several terms in common use for describing 12-tone music. Definitions of these are essential for further discussion; some of them represent only further clarification of notions we have already been using.

Pitch Class In Western music we use a continuum of pitches whose range has been slowly expanding since antiquity until, since the mid-nineteenth century, it occupies almost the whole audible spectrum of sound. This expansion of register as a historical process may be summarized roughly in the following diagram, which shows registral extremes for several periods of music history. Note also that until the Renaissance the range of an individual work was almost always less than that of music as a whole. This often remains true thereafter, but there also come into existence individual works that span the total gamut of pitches. In example 16, we show only approximate range, of *written* music, without regard for *ad hoc* doublings (boy sopranos, high recorders, etc.) in medieval and Renaissance music:

EXAMPLE 16

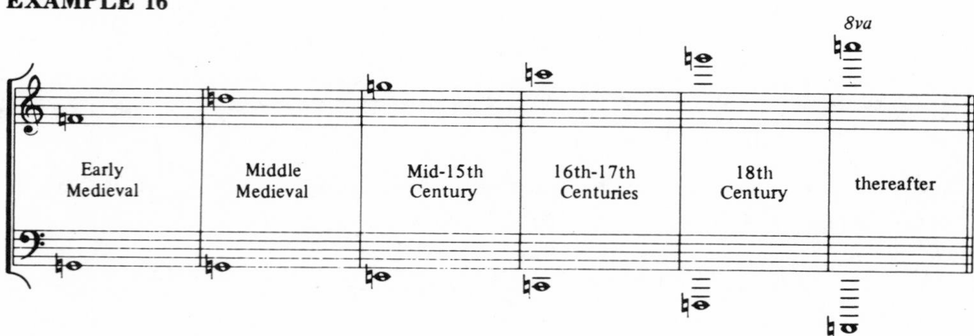

It seems that as the range occupied by the continuum of pitches expanded, the need for its internal organization grew progressively stronger. There appears to have developed an ever clearer sense of the continuum of pitches as divided into equal parts. Thus during the Renaissance the octave, which was originally regarded as consisting of two distinct pitch entities, came slowly to be heard as an interval consisting of two different expressions of the *same* entity.

Today, we think of the pitch continuum as divided up by groups of these "different expressions of the same entity"—as divided by octaves—and within each octave, we think of the same interval succession (the 12 half-steps) as being repeated. Of course, the positioning of these dividing octaves (i.e., what tone they begin on) is an arbitrary matter.

EXAMPLE 17 The Pitch Continuum

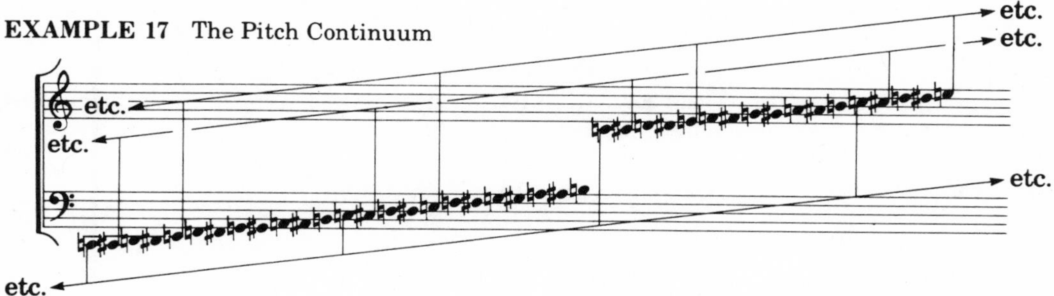

Moreover, since equal temperament was introduced (beginning in the eighteenth century), we have arranged the twelve half-steps within the octave itself into intervals of exactly equal size. We call the octave, since it divides all the tones of music into functionally equivalent groups, the *modular interval*; we consider all tones separated from each other by octaves to be functionally equivalent:

EXAMPLE 18

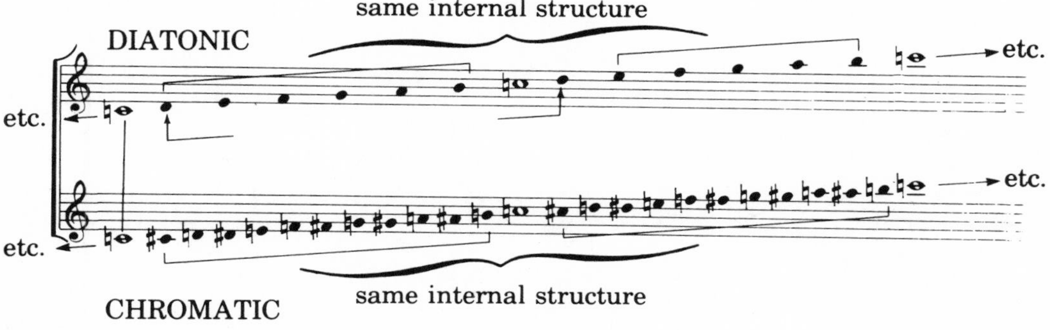

This attitude is reflected in our naming of tones: When we say "C-sharp," we refer to *all* C-sharps, and we know that the individual instances of C-sharp may be separated from each other by octaves. Tones that are related in this way we call members of the same *pitch class*. Thus, all D-naturals form a pitch class, as do all B-flats, etc. There are, obviously, twelve and only twelve distinct pitch classes: A, B-flat, B-natural, C, C-sharp, D, D-sharp, E, F, F-sharp, G, G-sharp, and their enharmonic equivalents. (Example 13, on page 22, represents an ordering of pitch classes.)

Therefore, for example, when we say that a piece is in C, we mean *pitch class* C and understand that the tonic can be expressed equally well by any specific C.

It is of the utmost importance to keep clearly in mind the distinction between *tones* and *pitch classes* (a distinction not made easier by our use of the word "pitch" to mean a specific tone). Tones are specific entities, representing and having exact and unique locations in the pitch continuum. Tones have *register*. Pitch classes are more abstract in nature, as they are classes of such entities. The distinction we are trying to emphasize is unfortunately not helped by our frequent practice of representing pitch classes in ordinary staff notation. For convenience, we often write tones on a staff when we are really thinking (compositionally or analytically) of pitch classes. Here we can only emphasize the distinction and urge the reader to take care with it:

EXAMPLE 19

Pitch classes notated on a staff:

Same pitch classes translated into actual notes in specific registers:

Moderato

Vc.

p

Register "Register" refers to more general locations in the pitch continuum than does "pitch." It may mean only a vague region, such as high, middle, or low; or it may refer to a tone's specific octave position:

EXAMPLE 20 Two Kinds of Register.

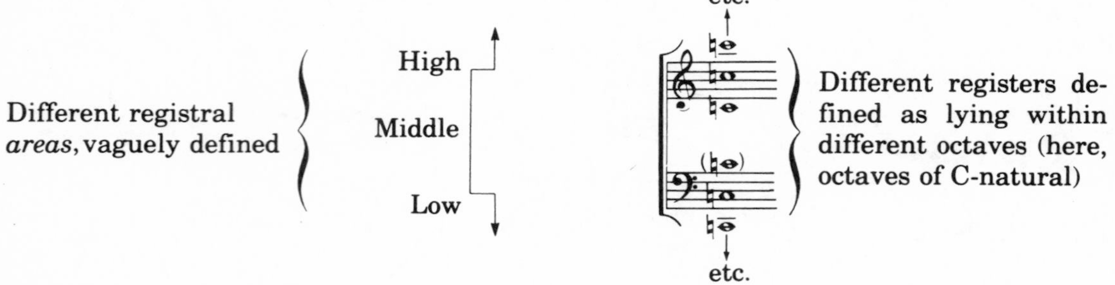

From this example, you can see that pitch classes are independent of register, since their members are defined as lying in different octaves. In the above example, there is only *one pitch class* represented—that of C-natural—but there are *five different tones*.

Octave Equivalence We have already defined this notion but include it here for completeness. It is the principle that tones separated by octaves are equivalent in function—whether in tonal music or in 12-tone music. (Another way of stating the same idea is to say that all members of the same pitch class are functionally equivalent.)

Set In ordinary language, this term means a collection (probably unordered) of similar things. In music, however, it has come to mean a collection of elements (usually pitch classes) possessing a specific ordering—and this will be our use of the term. The *ordering* is usually an ordering in time: One element comes first, another second, etc. But there are, of course, other ways to order the elements of a collection—by registral position, for instance, as shown in example 21:

EXAMPLE 21

A time ordering of pitch classes could be expressed as

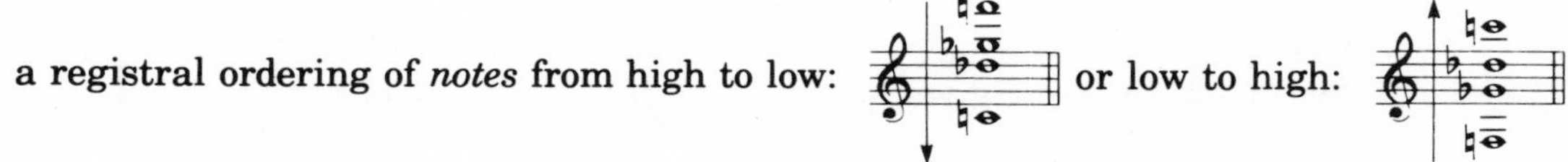

A mere unordered group of pitch classes is usually just called a *collection*, or sometimes a *content group*.

A set may contain any number of elements, and they need not all be unique. But by far the most common and important sets are *12-tone sets*, which are defined as containing each of the twelve distinct pitch classes once and only once in some time ordering. Thus, the number of elements in these sets is always twelve, the elements are always distinct from each other, and therefore no element is repeated. There are 479,001,600 (or 12!) possible orderings of twelve distinct elements, and therefore this is the number of possible 12-tone sets.

Various types of ordered sets of pitch classes are shown in example 22:

EXAMPLE 22

(a) Less than 12 elements without repetition:

(b) Less than 12 elements with repetition:

(c) A 12-tone set:

(d) More than 12 elements, therefore containing repetitions:

(e) A diatonic tune:

(f) The same tune abstracted into an ordered set:

Segment A name given (especially) to divisions of 12-tone sets, and usually consisting of adjacent elements. When the elements of the tone groups enumerated below are not adjacent, we speak of them as *partitions*.

If they consist of 2 tones, the segments are called *dyads*;
If they consist of 3 tones, the segments are called *trichords*;
If they consist of 4 tones, the segments are called *tetrachords*;
If they consist of 6 tones, the segments are called *hexachords*.

The above-named segments are shown in example 23-a;

EXAMPLE 23–a

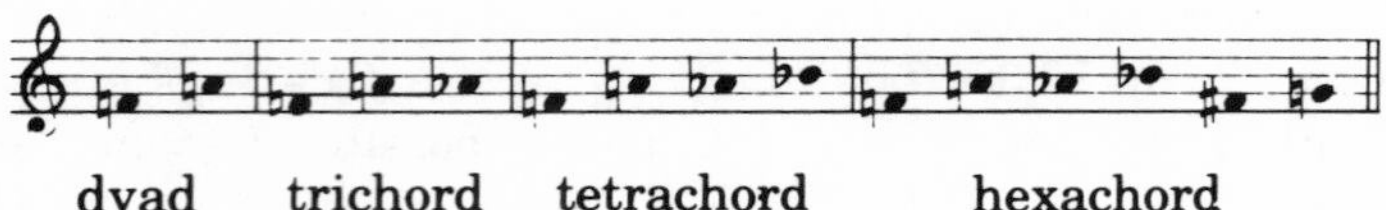

Note: 1. Segments of 5, 7, 8, or 9 elements are called pentads, heptads, octads, and nonads.
2. "Triad" (the Greek-derived form of the name for a 3-element group) is not used because of its special meaning in tonal music.

The segments listed in the table are by far the most important in the 12-tone world, since they are integral divisions of the total of twelve pitch classes. The other, unequally derived segments, are less important. Here is a 12-tone set with its various segmental divisions indicated:

EXAMPLE 23–b Set segments.

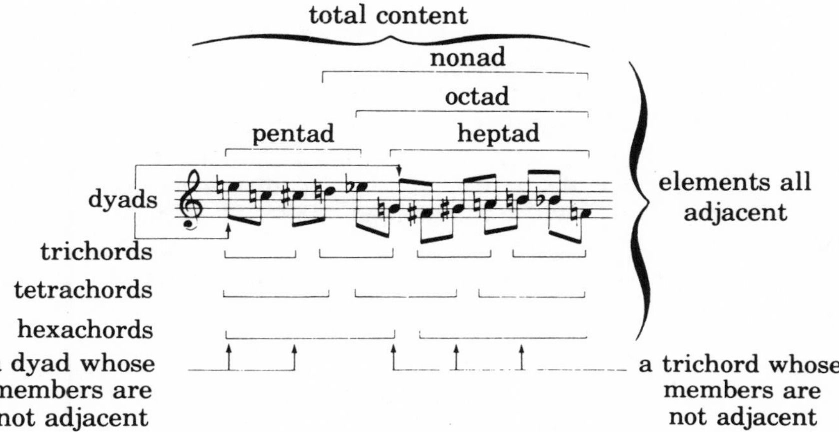

Total Chromatic This is the name we give to the total of the twelve distinct pitch classes. Thus, in a somewhat abstract way, it signifies the total pitch vocabulary of music. A 12-tone set is an ordered representation of the total chromatic. So is a chord containing all twelve pitch classes—and here the ordering is one of registral distribution. So, also, is a chord or succession that has all twelve pitch classes, with some of them repeated.

EXAMPLE 24

(a) A 12-tone chord made by disposing the first hexachord of Example 23-b upward, and the second downward.

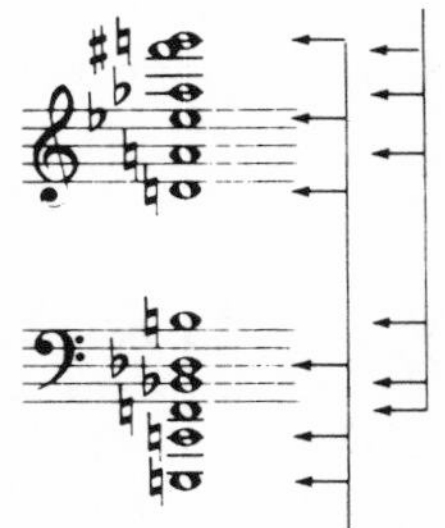

(b) Another 12-tone chord made from the two distinct whole-tone collections

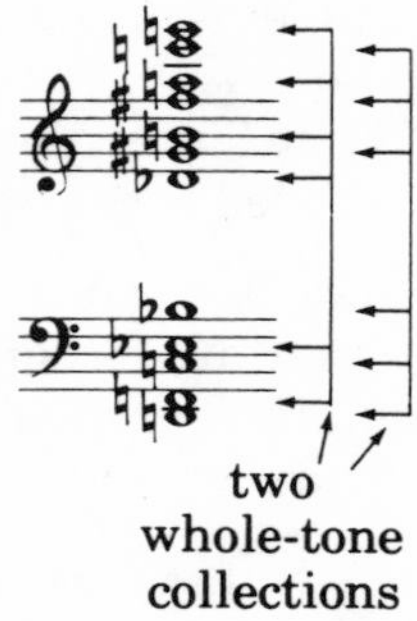

Operations Generally, in using this term, we refer to specific musical transformations carried out on collections of elements, which are most usually tones or pitch classes. Examples of such operations are: transposition, inversion, and retrogression. These, along with a few others, have fundamental importance in the 12-tone world, and we will define and discuss them later. For the moment, however, it suffices to have an idea of the notion of simply defined, repeatable processes which can be applied to various different collections without respect to the exact makeup and nature of the collections. Here, for instance, is transposition (denoted by T) applied to diatonic and chromatic collections:

EXAMPLE 25

(a) T:  in C major, under T_7 is transposed to G major (i.e., T by 7 semitones):

(b) The following 12-tone set:

is transposed under T_6 to:

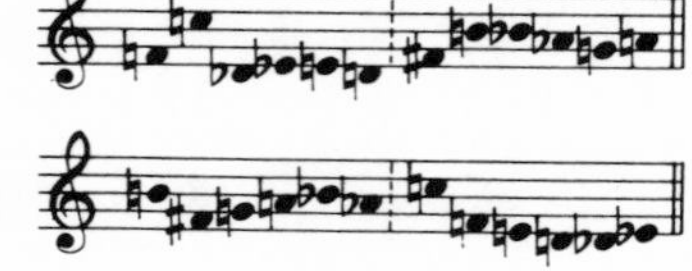

T_6 means transposition by six semitones, always under the convention that the interval of transposition is upward. (T_6 causes the content of the two hexachords in the set in example 25 to be exchanged—i.e., the pitch classes of the first become the pitch classes of the second. This pitch-class/content relation is a special property of this set; we mention it here only to anticipate a fuller discussion in chapter 9. Can you see the relation between the ordering of the first hexachord and that of the second?)

CHAPTER THREE

Surface

Music is certainly not a one-dimensional phenomenon, and one of the most remarkable things about it is that our sense of its multidimensionality comes from our reception of what is, acoustically, only one-dimensional. When we hear music, we are receiving a continuously fluctuating amplitude, yet at any one instant there is only one amplitude, for the eardrum can only be in one place at any one time. And yet we receive music in our ears and minds as filled with dimensionality: We hear and distinguish different instruments and individual notes (and we differentiate high from low tones with great precision), identify counterpoint, remember similarities, observe differences, and even remember and relate elements and events that are not adjacent to each other in the flow of time—all this from a single strand of sounds! This extraordinary capacity of ours to perceive music on so many levels (wresting multidimensionality out of what is really one-dimensional, acoustically) does not merely enable us to sort out and "analyze" music's surface characteristics; it also functions on a more fundamental, conceptual level as well.

When we hear even the simplest piece of music, we are aware of a sense of *depth;* that is, we not only identify the succession and combination of sounds in the immediate foreground, but also perceive a more deeply buried "background"—a more general and abstract network of relationships—out of which the immediate, local, and more superficial aspects of the composition seem to arise. Furthermore, we usually are aware of not just two layers of this sort, but rather a multiplicity of them, and they are not isolated from each other—in a good piece they are in lively communication.

This foreground we shall call the compositional "surface," and it is the recognition of a conceptual/perceptual distinction between it and the deeper structure of pieces that has led to the most fruitful attempts to "explicate" them analytically. Here, we are concerned with *composing* pieces, but we shall nevertheless find that the distinction is just as important for us as for an analyst. Let us examine this analytic process by applying it to a particular example.

final product. Since the instant-to-instant succession of happenings in a piece is best composed in response to local needs, there will always be a gap between structural principles that can be neatly outlined and described, and the answer to the crucial question of detail: What do I do next?

As an illustration of this relation, there follows an example of a miniature piece, with its structural scaffolding and generating principles stated first; then an unornamented version produced by the consistent application of the principles; and finally the complete piece, with its surface sufficiently ornamented. Note that the principle of surface articulation is intuitive, responding to immediate musical needs.

Suppose we decide to write a 12-tone phrase in moderate tempo for two violas. (This represents several basic decisions.) The total chromatic:

EXAMPLE 28–a

must be, by virtue of our decision to use the 12-tone system, ordered into a 12-tone set, and we decide on the following specific ordering:

EXAMPLE 28–b

which will be used for the piece. Next, we decide to combine two transformations of the whole set—the original and a transposed inversion—so that the first hexachords of each transformation together contain the twelve pitch classes. (This set displays certain special properties which will be discussed further on, in chapter 9.)

EXAMPLE 28–c

Since we have two set-forms, divided into halves, we will take the implication of the material to be that each of our two instruments will have one set-form to utter, and that the phrase we are to write will be articulated as a two-part affair:

EXAMPLE 28–d

Now we know who has what notes (or, more properly, pitch classes). Next we decide that Viola II will accompany Viola I, and make a rough sketch of the principal part, followed by a sketch of the accompaniment:

EXAMPLE 28–e

(The rhythm of the above is contextually and intuitively chosen.)

Finally, we revise registral values, ornament the rhythm a little, add dynamic and articulative indications:

EXAMPLE 28–f

And our task is complete.

Notice the following: if this had been a Mozart-style illustration, the organizing principles (shown in examples 28-a, 28-b, and 28-c) would have been those of the tonal system, and would not have been chosen by the composer himself. Virtually his entire task would lie in the "mere" completion of the surface. Since we no longer live in an age where basic musical structure and syntax is given *a priori* by convention, we must each choose our own organizing principles. *Not* to choose is to relegate the most difficult task in composition to the least articulate aspect of the mind: the semi-conscious, half-remembered, regurgitive function. In any case, we have a "freedom" denied our ancestors; but this freedom robs us of the "certainty" with which they could compose.

The compositional methods we shall describe later are useful because they generate the underlying skeleton of the work we are writing—most usually, successions and combinations of pitch classes, together with their locations in time, their *attack points*. But to make musical sense and significance of these, to render them *expressive* (of whatever the composer chooses, or his hearer wishes to invent), we first need some practical observations on the articulation of surface detail, so that when we describe these methods later, their generality and abstractness will not hinder their proper employment.

EXERCISES

1. Take example 28-f, page 39, and reduce it in the manner of examples 27-a–e (keeping the two voices separate throughout).
2. Using the same number of steps, do the same for the musical lines a, b, and c in the first exercise given on page 31 (chapter 2).
3. Compare the results of (1) and (2) above. Each musical line was composed with a 12-tone set. Yet your reduction in each case should show a different hierarchy of relations. Compare all of these with examples 28-a–f. Thus is composition different from analysis.
4. Take the reductions you made in (1) and (2) above. Re-express them as new lines, retaining the basic hierarchy of importance among the succession of pitch classes, but making the new lines as different in every respect (tempo, register, articulation, etc.) as you can. Thus can a single array of pitch class/attack point relationships be expressed in a multitude of ways.

CHAPTER FOUR

Rhythm

We have already seen that rhythm is not really a separable entity. A mere succession of attacks or pulses does not by itself define much of anything. But when rhythmic values are attached to different tones or other sounds, the picture changes. Here too, we have seen that the same succession of attacks, when invested with different series of pitches, acquires different meanings, as the following example illustrates:

EXAMPLE 29

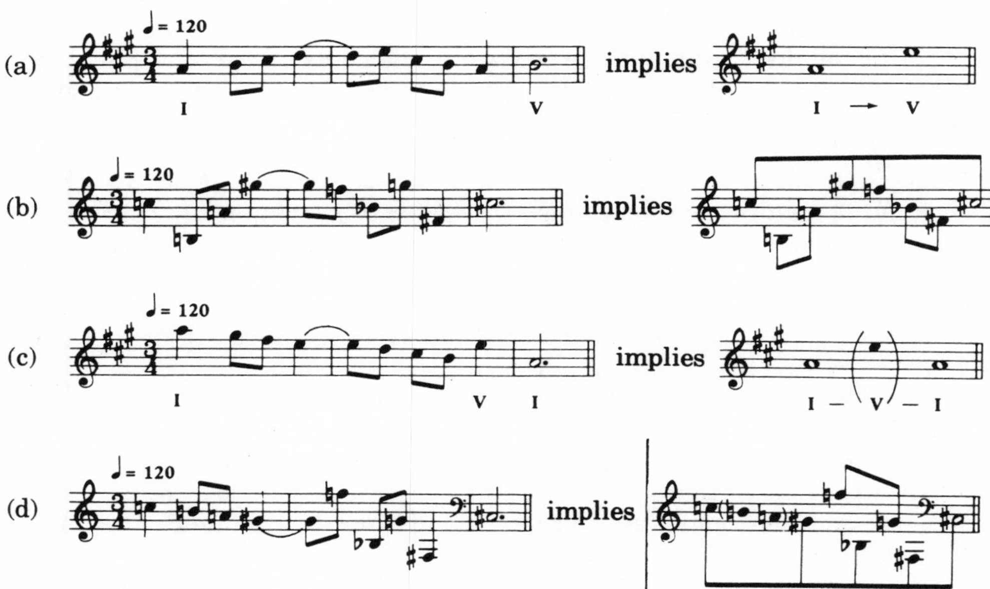

In each melodic line, the rhythm is the "same"; but notice how different the *sense* of each is, as expressed in the corresponding "analytic" reductions. In 29-a and 29-c, which are both tonal, the different harmonic implications resulting from the different successions of tones cause the same rhythmic succession to acquire structural points of stress in different places, thus changing the larger sense of the passage. In 29-b and 29-d, which are chromatic, the same succession of pitch classes is given two different registral interpretations; this causes differing registrally defined counterrhythms to be set up in the two cases and creates differing impressions of which tones are the most significant in the passage.

We should be well reminded by this that time and pitch are not independent of each other but interact in many important ways. We can consider this matter at many levels of generality, from the most detailed (as in example 29) to the most general (as when considering large-scale formal/gestural ideas as they are influenced by the harmonic unfolding of a work). First, however, let us address the question from the broadest point of view, by comparing the tonal (or diatonic) situation with that of the 12-tone (or chromatic).

Pitch relations in tonal music are characterized by asymmetry and inequality at every level, from the broadest sense of harmonic motion to the smallest element of surface detail. Inequality of importance in the respective functions of tones prevails throughout. There is one tone in the 3-tone tonic triad—the root—which is prime among the seven tones of the scale, and also among the twelve tones of the total chromatic. On the other hand, the rhythmic physiognomy of truly diatonic music is characterized by periodicity on at least one level.

In highly chromatic music, on the other hand, this relationship between pitch and rhythm seems to be reversed. Chromatic music, especially 12-tone, is characterized by the presence of all twelve elements of the total pitch class vocabulary nearly all the time, and as we have learned, this is why such music cannot be founded on principles of pitch content but must turn instead to ordering. We have, then, metaphorically, a homogeneous pitch class situation in chromatic music, and it is significant that the rhythmic structure of most such music features aperiodicity and irregularity in its unfolding. The intuitive sense of composers of increasingly chromatic music from Wagner onward has been to complement homogeneity within the pitch class hierarchy with rhythmic irregularity.

A caution here, before we proceed: When we talk about rhythm, we are speaking really about *interval*—in this case, *temporal interval*—just as we were really referring to pitch interval in our discussions of pitch. For it is the temporal distance between attacks (or other initiations of musical events) that we perceive as pulse, whether it is regular or irregular; the actual durations of the events whose initiations mark off the pulse are of far less significance. We shall see later how important this distinction is for the rhythmic organization of 12-tone composition.

To demonstrate, we present example 30, in which the pulse (i.e., the succession of temporal intervals) is the same in each case, while the durations of the component events are always different. Notice that here, far more than in the case of a succession of pitches whose durations remain the same while their registral positions are varied, the rhythm really seems the "same" in each representation:

EXAMPLE 30

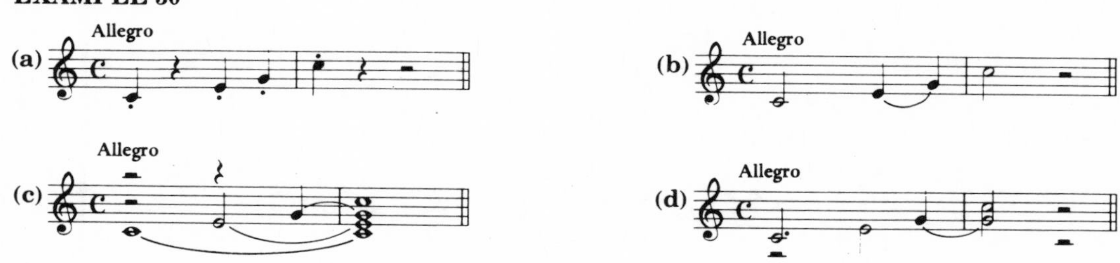

To what conclusions are we led? Clearly, it is not possible to prescribe every detail of rhythmic behavior, but we can at least offer a few general suggestions for making the rhythmic surfaces of 12-tone compositions. We advise a generous use of rhythmic aperiodicity, whether of meter, beat subdivision, foreground rhythm, or all of these in whatever combination. This of course does not mean that regular pulsation should always be avoided, but just as irregularity of pulse occurs as the exception in tonal music, so should regularity be the exception in chromatic music. Remember that anything exceptional calls attention to itself, and thus the occasional regularities of rhythmic flow that you may introduce into your compositions had better come at significant moments and not merely be tossed casually into the general continuity.

Sequential rhythmic repetition should be avoided. That is, in general one should not answer one clearly defined rhythmic/pitch gesture with another whose rhythmic unfolding is identical or nearly identical to the first. At the same time, however, antecedent/consequent phrase relations are useful and can be profitably employed. Bear in mind here, that even in tonal music the consequent had better not be too literal a repeat of the antecedent. How much more so is this true in 12-tone music! Here we are tempted to say that the question/answer bipartite phrase division inherited from the diatonic past should be regarded in a highly metaphorical way. Be careful not to go beyond approximate balancing of phrase halves, and avoid literal repetition.

The following will help to illustrate our precepts: The diatonic pitch succession:

EXAMPLE 31–a

will be better expressed rhythmically as:

EXAMPLE 31–b

than as:

EXAMPLE 31–c

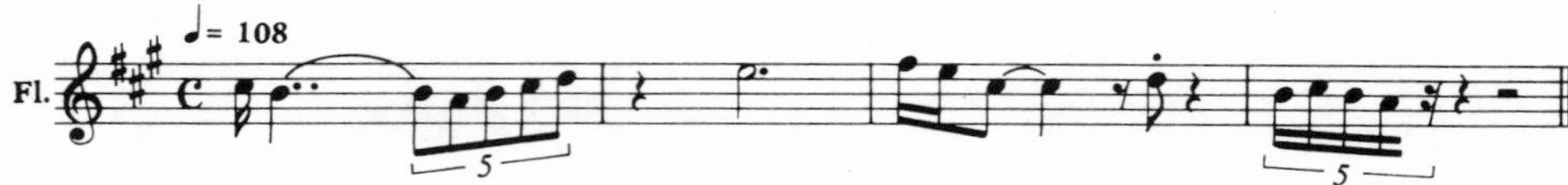

Conversely, the 12-tone pitch succession:

EXAMPLE 32–a

will go better as:

EXAMPLE 32–b

than as:

EXAMPLE 32–c

although certainly example 32-c is a less grotesque mismatch of rhythmic gesture to pitch unfolding than is example 31-c. (Refer back to the remarks on sequential repetition, above.)

In the discussion of rhythmic matters, we must draw a distinction between irregularity of meter and irregularity of metric subdivision—that is, between the succession of beats themselves, and the way in which the beats may be subdivided. Both kinds of rhythmic irregularity are useful in making and ornamenting the surface of a composition; and moreover, such patternings may have been the result in specific cases of more fundamental compositional operations. Some examples of rhythmic irregularity are given schematic rendering in example 33: (a) irregular meter but regular subdivision; (b) irregular subdivision but regular meter; and (c) both combined:

EXAMPLE 33

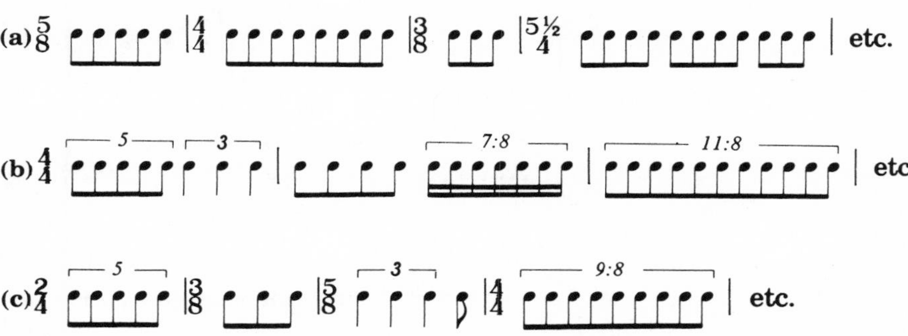

In looking at example 33, keep in mind that (1) what is represented are beats and subdivisions, not particular rhythmic patterns (actual rhythmic patterns could be made out of these, without necessarily using every subdivision of each beat); and (2) the notations 7:8 (read: seven in the time of eight), 11:8, and 9:8 indicate that seven, eleven, or nine eighths replace the usual eight eighths in the same time interval. This method of notating uneven subdivisions can be infinitely extended (5:4, 7:9, 4:3, etc.). There are several other current ways of showing the same thing, but this method is the clearest and most widely adopted.

A succession of equal, stressed *beats* will of course tend to establish a sense of periodicity and regularity even if the internal subdivisions of each beat are different from those of their surroundings. So, likewise, will a succession of unequal beats or measures, if the minimum subdivision unit is actually expressed and is held constant. These conditions are illustrated in example 34:

EXAMPLE 34 Periodicity.

(a) Equal beats,* unequal subdivisions:

(b) Variable beat, single constant subdivision:

*which may or may not be organized into measures of changing size

From the combination of these possibilities, one may choose the degree of rhythmic regularity, or periodicity, that one finds appropriate to specific compositional situations. Here it is of primary importance to note that the pitch system used for the composition—regardless of the pitch system's characteristics—will take on more and more the characteristics of a pitch-*centric* system, the more regular its rhythmic unfolding is made to be. (Pitch-centric systems elect a given tone or group of tones as a fundamental reference point; the best example is that of the election of one tone as the tonic in the tonal system.) This is why certain 12-tone pieces whose rhythmic surfaces are—inappropriately—too regular, seem so "dissonant": not because consonance and dissonance have any objective meaning apart from their functionally defined roles in tonal music, but rather because a freely circulating chromatic pitch flow is being mismatched with a regular and homogeneous rhythmic flow. This causes the hearer to hierarchize strong beats as *pitch*-relationally significant, and (by association as much as anything else) to expect from the chromatic notes attached to these "diatonic" rhythms a functional hierarchy like that of tonal music. When this expectation is frustrated, it leads to a sense that the music is incoherent.

We should make another observation here as well: The effect of tempo on the kinds of rhythmic unfolding we have been suggesting is very marked. In most of these, we have assumed a moderate-to-fast rate of unfolding, because it is in these speeds that periodicities (i.e., the perception of larger units of temporal succession) are most readily perceived. In slower tempi, regularity is much less obtrusive, unless it is insisted upon through articulative means (e.g., funereal bass drum thumps). So our suggestions regarding rhythm should be understood to apply in varying degrees as the rate of unfolding varies, being most necessary at the fastest tempi, and least at slow tempi.

The periodic/aperiodic continuum can furnish a composer with a range of choice as to just where on the scale from diatonic tonality to freely circulating chromaticism he wishes to locate his piece; and these relations are yet another hint that the tonal and 12-tone systems are part of a larger, unified whole.

EXERCISES

1. Notate appropriate rhythmic expression for the following pitch successions:

(a)

(b)

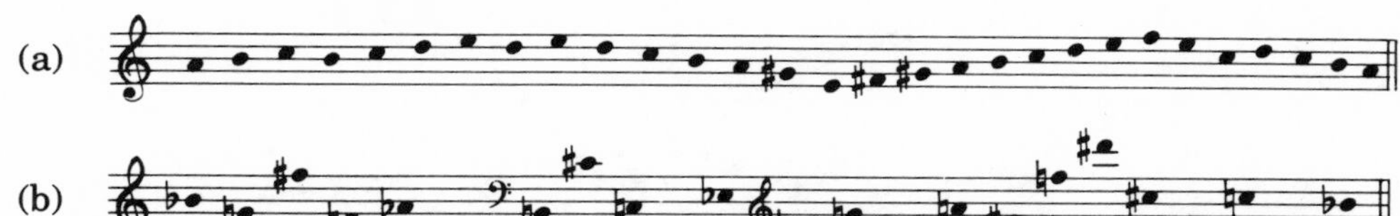

(c)

2. For each of the following pitch-*class* successions, make two different rhythmic expressions. In each case: first make registral choices; then attach rhythmic values. The two versions of each succession should not come out rhythmically the same:

(a)

(b)

(c)

3. Given the following rhythmic patterns, find pitch successions appropriate to the degree of regularity represented in each case:

(a) ♩ = 96 4/4 etc.

(b) ♩. = 72 12/8 etc.

(c) ♩ = 120 5/8 2/4 4/4

(d) ♩ = 160 3/8 7/8 6/16 3/8 7/8

(e) ♩ = 108 4/4

The following examples are possible beginnings for some of the exercises above:

for 1. (a)

for 2. (b)

for 3. (a)

(c)

CHAPTER FIVE

Melody

Melodic Construction

What is melody? This is one of many dubious questions, debated over the centuries by critics, aestheticians, and those hostile to changes in compositional method or intent. As everyone knows, the question is usually raised not in order to demonstrate that something *is* melody but rather that it isn't. We shall not presume to enter these metaphysical realms. For us, melody means *tune*—a linear pitch/rhythmic succession whose contour and articulation set it apart from its surroundings and entitle us to perceive it and think of it as a separate entity.

It is my conviction that twentieth-century musical thought has generalized the notion of melody. As to this, what has happened in music is perhaps not unlike what has occurred in other fields, such as the sciences, in which our age has witnessed the making of "universals" out of what were formerly aggregations of special cases. By our lights, for example, a melody need no longer be confined to a single voice or instrument—it may be divided up among many. (This is a common practice throughout twentieth-century music. In light-textured music, such as Webern's, it has been described by the unfortunate term "pointillism," borrowed inappropriately from the field of painting.) Moreover, as we shall see momentarily, modern melody usually covers a far wider registral range than did its diatonic ancestors, and this has a double consequence. First, it blurs the distinction between melody and accompaniment, should there be any. Second, and more important, in contrapuntal circumstances it creates a network of intersecting, registrally overlapping lines. These conditions are the inevitable result of the registral expansion of individual lines: The more room they take up in the audible pitch space, the more they will have to invade each other's territory. Finally, the aperiodic nature of the rhythm of chromatic music (we refer the reader to chapter 4) makes the unfolding of present-day lines less given to obvious sectional division (literally balanced antecedents and consequents) than was diatonic melody.

In example 35, we illustrate a rough correlation between the degree of chromaticism in the lines presented and the registral space they require for their clear expression. The more chromatic, the wider the total range:

EXAMPLES 35a–c

Taking example 35-c and "flattening" it out, notice how much less well-defined and "independent" each interval becomes when the tune is registrally more confined:

EXAMPLE 35–d

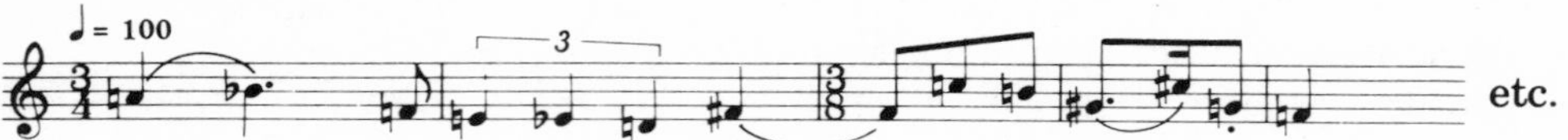

The observation of the changes brought about in the tune through this act of registral confinement can lead us to a more general formulation of the main characteristics of melody in 12-tone or otherwise highly chromatic pieces. The following principles of melodic construction as developed for diatonic melody (first modal, then later tonal) hold in a general way for chromatic melody too:

1. Rhythmic and registral balance should be maintained between or among the major divisions of the line (particularly antecedent/consequent balance).
2. Not too many notes (that is, not too many intervals) are to be taken in the same direction without compensatory change in the opposite direction.
3. A general balance should be maintained between upward- and downward-directed movement, this of course modified by whether or not the general tendency of the line is to end higher, lower, or in the same region as it started.

But there is one critical difference between chromatic and diatonic melody: The registral range of non-tonal melody must be substantially wider than that for tonal melody. We have already learned that this is essential for the clear presentation of the interval successions of chromatic melody, whose ordering is what gives such melody its coherence, expressiveness, and force. There is, however, one modification to this precept: The registral range is often a function of tempo; that is, the slower the tempo, the more confined the melody may (but of course not necessarily *must*) be. This is because when there is greater time distance between attacks, the succession of intervals is easier to hear as a string of independent pitch distances, and therefore the succession-clarifying leaps and changes of direction so essential in faster tempi can be dispensed with.

The issues we have raised here might be clarified by considering the following diagram. In this representation of a three-dimensional "co-ordinate space," one axis shows the degree of registral dispersion, another the tempo, and a third the type of music.

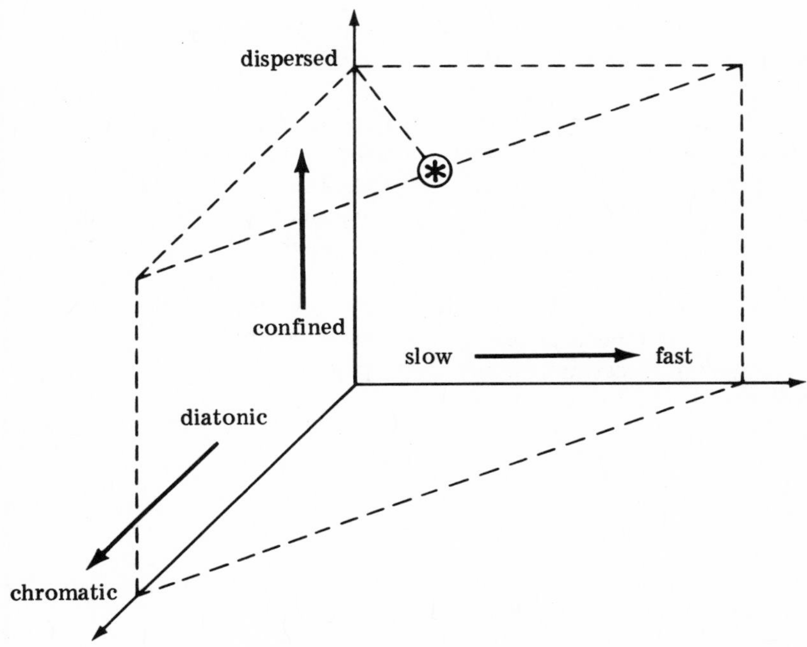

The point marked with an asterisk represents a viable relation between fast unfolding and wide registral dispersion for a melodic line in a 12-tone piece.

The reason that chromatic melody is more disjunct than diatonic melody, then, lies in the domain of fundamental pitch relations. In tonal music, coherence is achieved by asserting pitch/interval *content*; in order to hear a tonal melody, therefore, one needs most basically to be aware of its interval content. For this recognition to be accomplished, it is advantageous (though by no means always obligatory) to have registral confinement as the norm for the definition of the line's contour.

Example 36 shows a tonal tune, first in what one could regard as a "normal" registral distribution, then in an "abnormal" one with the registral range expanded by means of selected octave displacements:

EXAMPLE 36

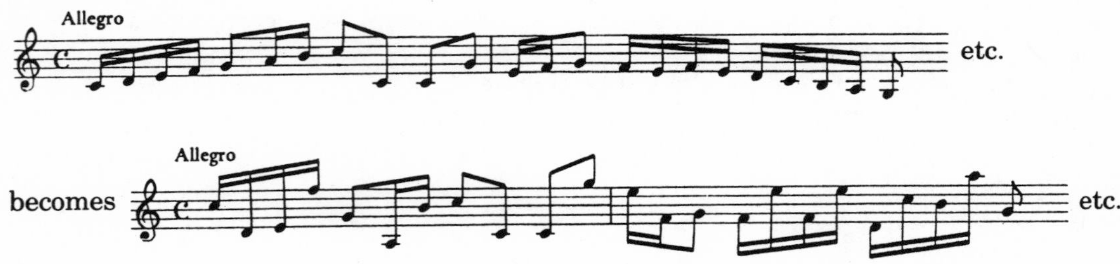

Notice how the recognition of interval content becomes more difficult as the range and frequency of leaps increases. Notice too that "normal" large tonal leaps are most often octaves. Here the gestural difference achieved by the leap is compensated for by the fact that the pitches involved are identical, in terms of pitch class. Finally, notice that in our disjunct version, the leaps tend to set up misleading emphases and counterrhythms which contradict the basic harmonic motion of the passage.

However, in chromatic music, as we know, one depends on hearing interval *order,* since content perception alone yields nothing special. Thus, we must hear the interval succession as clearly as possible.

EXAMPLE 37–a

Example 37-a shows a large interval bracketing two smaller ones. Unless some non-registral means (such as rhythm) is used to emphasize the smaller intervals, the interval from C-natural to A-natural will appear the most significant of the three, the intervals C-natural to G-sharp and G-sharp to A-natural remaining incidental. Now if the point (as in the expression of a 12-tone set) is to hear C-natural to G-sharp *and* G-sharp to A-natural as independent and equal, then we cannot retain the same direction and registral area for the interval from G-sharp to A-natural. We need to make some kind of change there—perhaps take the A-natural down an octave:

EXAMPLE 37–b

The requirement to hear interval successions clearly in 12-tone music can be met only by frequent changes of linear direction; and this in turn leads to frequent use of "leaps"—especially compounds of the smaller intervals (minor ninths and major sevenths for minor seconds, etc.), and even of larger ones as well (perfect twelfths for perfect fifths, etc.). It is from this pitch-relational requirement that the registral, and therefore the gestural, nature of chromatic music arises; and for diatonic melody, the contrary pitch-relational requirement has had its effect. In fact, the tradition of non-disjunct (primarily stepwise) melodic progression in diatonic music has been so strong that the very term "melody" has to many ears meant exclusively non-disjunct motion. Disjunct linear motion, therefore, has often been a signal to critics that "melody" is absent.

EXAMPLE 38–a

In example 38-a, each successive interval moves in a different direction from either of its neighbors; thus, for instance, even though the B-flat is only a sixteenth-note, the F-natural/B-flat interval is clearly expressed. On the other hand, if the same pitch-class succession were registrally confined, the B-flat would become merely an incident on the way to A-natural:

EXAMPLE 38–b

In this second version, then, changing the B-flat to some other tone (say, B-natural) would have far less pitch-relational effect than it would in the original version (i.e., example 38-a), because the B-flat has been diminished in importance by its registral position. (Of course, we could emphasize the B-flat by giving it longer duration, but that would be a rhythmic change, which is more fundamental than a registral change, and not within the limits of our example.)

EXERCISES

1. The following lines are written arbitrarily in close registral distribution, without regard to intervallic needs. By selecting new registral positions for as many of the tones as you please, make the lines into melodies, using a full registral distribution and appropriate dynamics and articulation for the designated instruments (and due regard for their ranges!).

2. Do the same as in exercise (1), above, for these next three lines, but now also decide tempo.

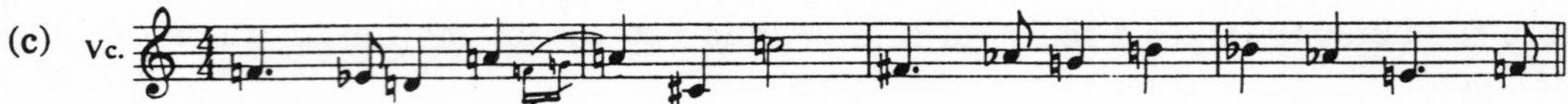

3. Do the same as in exercise (2) for these last four lines, but now also provide rhythmic values.

(c) Fl.

Chord Tone Distribution

A chief miracle of music lies in the way simultaneous and successive pitch relations can be made to harmonize in their unfolding: lines which are independent (in their articulation and contour) can be combined so that the tones simultaneously sounding support those successively sounding, and vice versa. Long before Schoenberg made his famous remarks about the identification of the horizontal and vertical dimensions in music, a deep awareness of this interdependency had developed in modal, and later tonal, music. For in music based on functionally defined consonance and dissonance, most intervals that function as consonances in successions do so in simultaneities (chords) as well. Thus, thirds, perfect fifths, sixths, and of course octaves, are consonances both as simultaneous and successive intervals; so too, with qualifications, is the perfect fourth; and while seconds are chordally dissonant but melodically consonant, they have a chordal function too, in their verticalization within seventh chords. And tritones, sevenths, ninths, etc., are dissonant both in chords and in melodies.

It should be no surprise, then, that a similar situation should prevail in music based upon interval *order*. Here, indeed, the interidentification of horizontal and vertical musical dimensions is even more complete than with diatonic music: There are no specific intervals or interval classes that are admissable as one function in the horizontal, and another in the vertical dimension. What is ordered successively can also be ordered simultaneously, but the means are different in the two cases. With lines, temporal ordering must be employed; in chords, spatial (i.e., registral) ordering must be used.

EXAMPLE 39

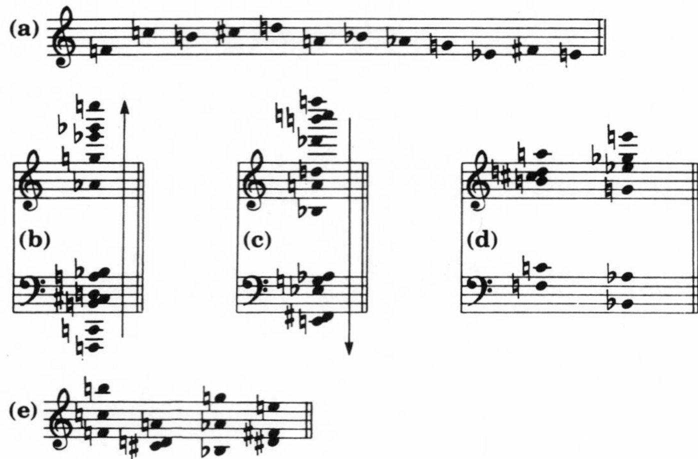

Thus, the pitch-class succession which is time-ordered (example 39-a) can be registrally ordered as a simultaneity (example 39-b). In example 39-b, the ordering is bottom to top; it can often be the other way, top to bottom (example 39-c). Comparing example 39-b and 39-c, notice that the intervals of one ordering (upward) are complements of the intervals of the other (downward). Of course, the two kinds of ordering may also be combined. In example 39-d, the two hexachords of the original set are registrally ordered as simultaneities, but their succession is a temporal ordering. If we carry this idea further, for instance with trichords (example 39-e), we begin to approach the situation of segmentally unordered sets, which we have already discussed in chapter 2—for here the number of elements in each simultaneity is so small that we do not need internal (registral) ordering to identify the interval content, which is recognizable without it.

Therefore, in the simple case of our merely wishing to present as simultaneously ordered what has already been successively ordered, we need only substitute registral order for temporal order. (See the previous examples.) But as we can imagine, this is only the most rudimentary, and therefore the least musically interesting, of possibilities. We need a more subtle means for translating the ordering of lines into the ordering of chords. For this, we must remember what ordering is *for:* In music based on interval order, it is to project as clearly as possible the complete intervallic fabric, thereby establishing the special intervallic personality possessed by each work that is based on interval order.

The need for expressing clearly the temporal ordering of intervals in the composing of lines has led us to make use of the registral dispersion tactics described at the beginning of this chapter. Now in the expression of chords, we ought to base our decisions on the actual *melodies* we have been making, rather than just the interval order of their successive tones. In other words, we should express simultaneously the registral choices appropriate to the pitch classes of our chord, as if it had started life as a line. (This is "gathering," the reverse of arpeggiation.) In doing this, we are not only carrying on relatively recent tonal traditions, in which chords arose by the elision of contrapuntal phenomena; reaching back somewhat further in history, we are generating our simultaneities in close analogy to the way in which chordal consciousness first arose out of the contrapuntal Renaissance (a development that is demonstrated diagrammatically in example 40).

EXAMPLE 40

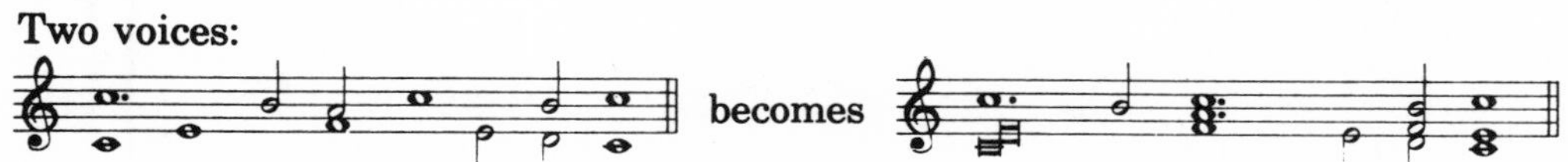

What we can do, therefore, is to regard simultaneities as *projections* onto the vertical dimension of what was previously a horizontal temporal ordering, clarified by appropriate registral choice for its constituent pitch classes. Let us try this with two of the lines we composed in the preceding section. First, the melodic line of example 35-c,

EXAMPLE 35-c

when made into a two-chord succession, becomes:

EXAMPLE 41

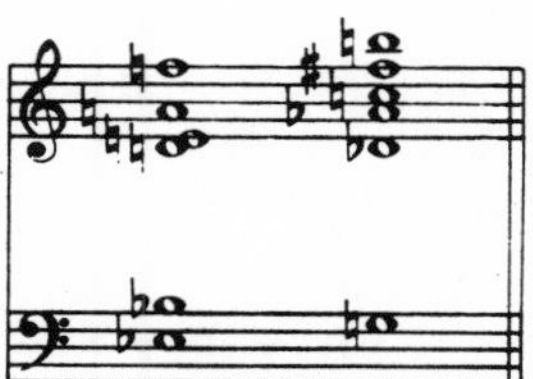

Here we have kept all the registers of the original line fixed, except for the C-sharp, which has been lowered one octave to avoid creating the interval of a minor second with the C-natural. This is done because the smallest intervals are hard to hear clearly in a context of many tones; the interval class C-sharp/C-natural sounds better as a seventh than as a second. Using the same procedure, example 38-a:

EXAMPLE 38–a

becomes:

EXAMPLE 42

Again there is only one registral change, for a similar reason—the B-natural has been lowered one octave.

In a way, the result of this procedure leads to a kind of content-oriented musical situation. But the road traveled to reach it is far different from the "straight" one of merely denying the significance of order. In the formation of a melodic line—38-a in this case—the registral positions of the successive tones are chosen in strict accordance with the need to express their interval order clearly (a principle discussed above, page 52). In projecting this line into a simultaneity, we are only producing, as it were, a derivative (or second-order) ordering.

But composing, subject as it is to so many mysterious influences, can rarely proceed with any degree of artistic success by means so fully automatic as those I have just described. Usually, when melodic lines are turned into simultaneities, some sort of registral adjustment is necessary, and our examples have already shown this. Thus, if we compress the melodic line of example 43-a:

EXAMPLE 43–a

into three chords of five, four, and three tones, respectively:

EXAMPLE 43–b

each of the chords will require alterations—mostly the first, since it is the least disjunct in its linearized form, the other two chords requiring only one registral change each (example 43-c):

EXAMPLE 43–c

Even though these chords are *internally* acceptable with only the minor changes that have been made, their *successional* relationship will be improved when they are altered further (example 43-d):

EXAMPLE 43–d

In this last stage of our example, the lowest notes of each chord form a "better" linear shape in registral terms than do the corresponding notes in its preceding stage.

Of course, we do not often wish to make melodic lines first and then gather their successive attacks together into chords; normally, we produce chords directly. Nevertheless, the principles outlined above will apply no matter which approach is taken. Referring our practices once more to tradition: Just as diatonic melody was usually made up of small intervals, so diatonic harmony usually made use of chords in close registral position—i.e., also small intervals—below the soprano. We might then say that the same underlying acoustically determined principles of chord formation that were developed in diatonic music apply here as well. In deciding how to order the tones of a chord, choose the intervals as you would if they made up a melodic line, and, in most instances, place the widest intervallic space at the lower end of the chord. Example 43-d shows the principle of placing the widest intervallic space at the lower end of the chord in the first and last chords, but not in the middle one. I exchanged the two lowest tones of the middle chord—C-natural and D-natural—from example 43-c to 43-d in order to improve the bass line progression, even though this alteration placed the largest interval between the two middle tones rather than the two lower ones; principles of good melodic construction take precedence.

EXERCISES

1. Make a single simultaneity of each of the following lines in two ways: First, translate the temporal ordering strictly into registral ordering, transforming first-to-last into low-to-high; second, preserving the original registral positions of the notes in the lines. Assign the duplicated notes in 1(c) to the same register:

2. Turn the following chords into melodic lines, in two stages: First write out each chord as an arpeggiation, preserving the given registral values of the constituent tones; then re-register the resulting succession, choosing appropriate rhythm, instrumentation, dynamics, etc.:

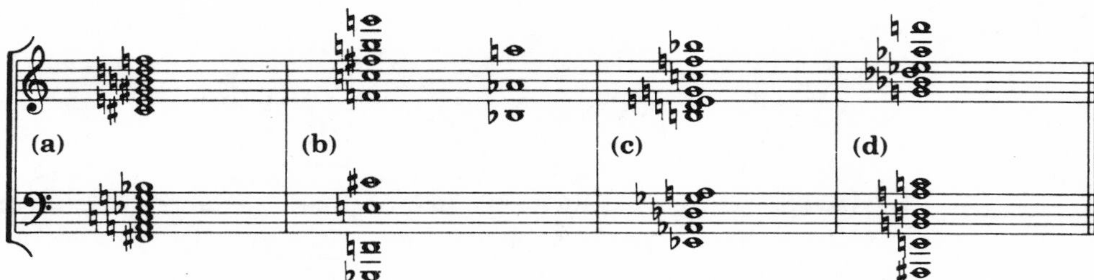

3. "Verticalize" the following pitch-class successions, in chords of three, four, and five tones. Make your own registral choices, but preserve the original temporal ordering, now translating it into registral ordering from high to low. Then make a second version of your chords, revising the registral position of the constituent tones for maximum intervallic clarity:

4. Make melodic lines out of the second version of chords generated in the preceding exercise. Translate registral ordering of the chords, reading from low to high, into temporal ordering; provide rhythm, registral variety within the line, articulation, etc. Compare the new successions of notes with those originally given in the preceding exercise.

Voice Leading

Having demonstrated how, just as with diatonic music, chords and lines in chromatic music function by sharing similar registral principles, it remains only to combine the two to arrive at principles of proper voice leading. If we regard the registral values assigned to lines or chords as extensible to combinations of lines, chords, or both, we will follow the same precepts, but only generalize the field of their application. Thus, two lines that are satisfactory individually are combined in example 44-a into an acceptable contrapuntal totality:

EXAMPLE 44–a

(This example simply combines the lines from examples 35-c and 38-a.)

Now we shall display a chord combined with a line:

EXAMPLES 44b–e

Here in example 44-b we have verticalized the first six notes of the top line of our newly made duet (shown in their original registral positions in example 44-c) and used them to accompany a melody formed by combining that line's remaining three notes (example 44-d) with the last three notes of the bottom line (example 44-e), thus making a complete expression of the total chromatic. Notice that although the chord preserves the same relative registral positions that its notes occupied when they were part of a line, it has been lowered an octave in order to get it clear of the melodic line it accompanies.

Example 44-f combines two 3-tone chords, whose tones are taken from the melody in example 44-b:

EXAMPLE 44–f

The two chords are combined into a single 6-tone chord, and in this operation, it is necessary to lower the C-sharp one octave to provide clear and even intervallic distribution.

From this, we may enunciate a general principle of contrapuntal combination: If all the tones of all the prospective constituents have registral positions that are satisfactory in a verticalization, they will also be acceptable in a contrapuntal combination.

On this principle, the two 6-tone chords in example 45-a can be made into, say, three lines (example 45-b), with the constituent tones remaining in the same registral positions they occupied in the chords:

EXAMPLES 45a–b

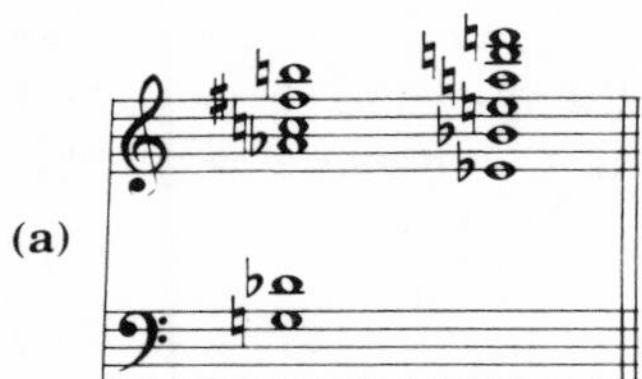

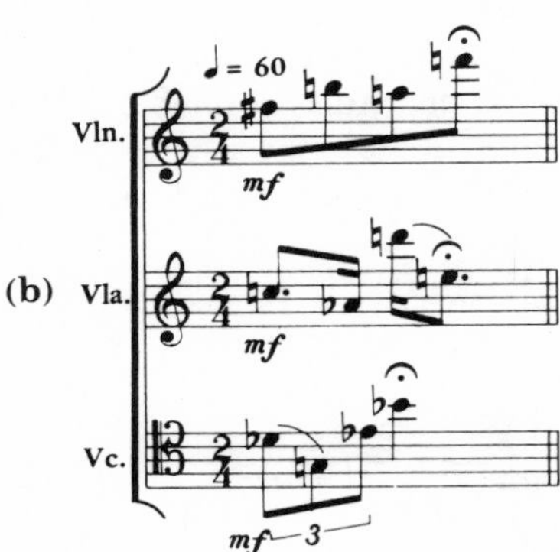

However, the converse of this principle does not necessarily hold; successful registration of counterpoint usually cannot be carried over directly into verticalization without registral adjustment. Thus, example 45-c is not especially good when verticalized as example 45-d. The second chord in example 45-d is acceptable, but the first needs registral dispersion to make its constituent intervals easier to hear, as in example 45-e:

EXAMPLES 45c–e

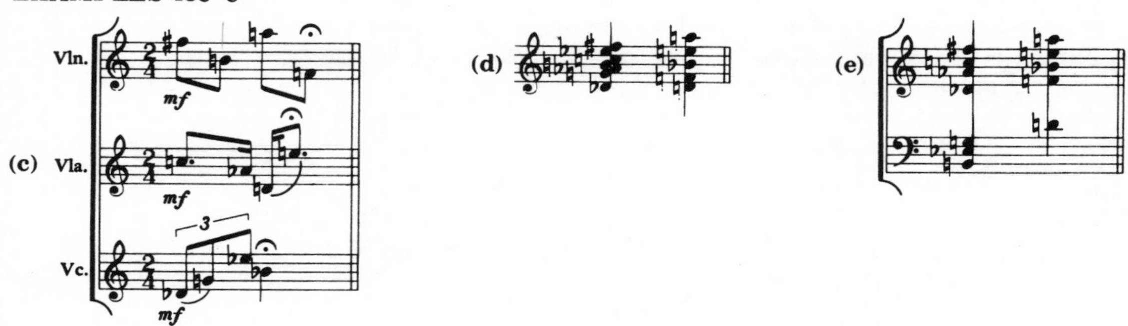

Notice something else of great compositional significance: Once the original constituents of a contrapuntal fabric have been combined according to the general principle given above, their several tones may be given new roles in new voices—that is, new linear paths may be traced through the whole array of pitches in their total temporal ordering; or, as we say, new lines may be *partitioned* out of the array. There are many uses for this device (and as we shall see in part III, it has great importance for the structure of the 12-tone system as an independent musical construction). Among other things, it can:

1. reinterpret a previously composed contrapuntal fabric;
2. turn monody into counterpoint;
3. reduce counterpoint to a single line; and so forth.

To illustrate point (1), let us change the three-voice counterpoint of example 45-b into four-voice counterpoint. In this process, we preserve the temporal and registral positions of each of the original notes. The change from three to four voices is effected simply by assigning each new attack to a new voice (in this operation, we read simultaneous attacks from highest pitch to lowest).

EXAMPLE 46

(N.B. Under ordinary circumstances, the last two notes in the cello part would probably be played as harmonics. They are written as natural notes here to make the pitches easier to read.)

Next, to illustrate point (2), let us write out first the constituent tones of the chords in example 45-a, translating their registral ordering, low to high, into temporal ordering, via arpeggiation:

EXAMPLE 47–a

This single strand of pitches we now partition into three voices, again assigning each new attack to a new voice, in order:

EXAMPLE 47–b

To illustrate point (3), let us combine the three voices of example 45-b into a single "line" (i.e., notating the exact order and rhythm in which the tones would be *sounded* by the three instruments playing together, to make a new composite line for a single instrument), thus obliterating contrapuntal distinctions. Note that this new line will, of necessity, include some simultaneities. As before, we have preserved the temporal and registral positions of the original:

EXAMPLE 48

Note also that the reduction of duplets and triplets necessitates the use of their least common multiple, sextuplets.

In its many applications, partitioning is not restricted to actual tones. Indeed, its more general uses can be found in the slicing of subsidiary entities out of arrays of pitch *classes*. In these usually more fundamental operations, registral position has no direct role. As with our examples, the registral values of the original material may be irrelevant or unsuitable for the new entity being produced by partitioning. In partitioning, the tones being processed are to be regarded as representatives of pitch classes and in the new entity are to be given new registral positions as the new situation warrants.

EXERCISES

A. Combining

1. Describe the relation between the following two voices:

What does the pitch succession of each voice consist of? Now, realign the two voices: (a) with Voice 1 starting one beat early, i.e.:

(a) 1. 3
2. 8

and (b) with Voice 1 starting one beat late, i.e.:

Now, rebar these two variants so that in each case, Voice 1 starts on the downbeat, i.e.:

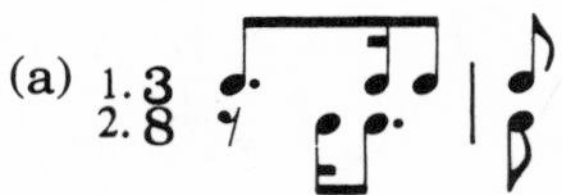

How does this shift of accent affect the pitch relationships on the passage? Are registral changes needed in view of the metric displacement?

2. Combine the following into three voice counterpoint, making appropriate registral choices for clarity of interval succession:

(a) What do you notice about the pitch-class content of each measure in the polyphonic result? (b) Within each measure of each voice separately? (c) The pitch-class successions are by content group, without internal ordering. List the content groups for each voice, for each measure. (In this, consider the F-sharp upbeat in the cello's first bar and the F-sharp upbeat in the violin's second bar as belonging to the next measure.) (d) What is the pitch-class content of each line?

B. Partitioning

Consider the following passage:

1. Reduce it to two voices, making necessary registral changes, by assigning alternate successive attacks to each voice. For simultaneities, read from the highest pitch down. A possible beginning is:

2. Reduce the passage to a single "line":

In making your conversion, reduce duple and triple subdivisions to a common rhythm, e.g.:

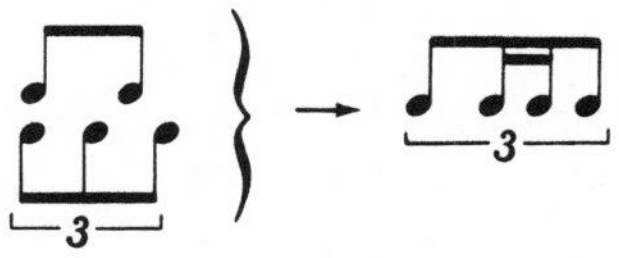

(N.B. In doing the reductions for both of the above exercises, heed the following advice:

—Regard simultaneous attacks in the original as belonging to a single voice. This is a shorthand way of expressing the fact that the simultaneously attacked pitches no longer belong to separate contrapuntal voices.

—Even though the voices may overlap, try to keep their *average* distance at least half an octave from each other.)

3. Now expand the monophonic succession that you made in Exercise (2), above, into four-voice counterpoint, for example starting:

Question What do you notice about the pitch-class content of each measure in these exercises?

CHAPTER SIX

Revision

It frequently happens that the results of compositional effort require repair and revision. This unhappy condition may arise because of: (1) some fault in the basic premises of the piece (for instance, a faulty pitch/rhythmic successional scheme); (2) inadequate or incomplete realization of the fundamental premises; or (3) incompleteness of editing, instrumentation, articulation, and so forth. The last of these three possibilities belongs properly to a more superficial, editorial phase of composing than the one we are discussing in this Part. The first is more fundamental (the pitch-class succession given in example 49 is perhaps the simplest instance of this kind of weakness, for it is easy to see that a work based on such a set is not likely to lead to much of interest:

EXAMPLE 49

We shall examine the more complex implications of this problem later on). The second, however, touches directly on our present subject—the sounding surface of compositions.

Let us suppose that the succession of notes and attack points (i.e., the basic pitch-class/rhythmic material) for a certain piece are accepted as given. In the kind of composing discussed in this book, it will normally be the case that such a succession, usually presented in terms of neutral pitch classes and attack points (that is, without registral values for the pitch classes, and without notating the duration of a given tone, only its point of initiation), will have arisen in the compositional process before the need comes to focus on precise registral, durational, contrapuntal, instrumental, articulative, and dynamic decisions. Let us assume anyway that these last-enumerated decisions have been made, at least tentatively. Are they satisfactory? That can be judged by applying the considerations for voice leading and related matters that we have just been discussing. If the decisions and their results are found repellent or diffuse or nondescript, what can be done to re-evaluate and repair them?

For the process of revision to be effective, we must first establish a clearly defined hierarchy of remedies. Furthermore, they must be arranged in a sensible order of application; otherwise, the process of revision may be ineffective, or, worse, may undermine the fundamental materials and relationships which have already been produced. Therefore one ought, on the one hand, to avoid beginning the work of revision with trivial alterations (such as surface-level juggling of dynamics, for example), and on the other, to postpone major surgery on the fundamental materials (pitch-class and rhythmic successions, most usually—but perhaps also including other basic characteristics of the piece, such as instrumental roles, text-setting in vocal works, dramatic requirements in theatrical works, and so forth) until the need for it is unmistakably established.

Register

In the search for a centrally located starting point, our attention might naturally turn toward registral values. These embody a paradox that clearly shows the fundamental difference between the compositional act and the perceptual process. In actual *composing,* register is far less important a value than is pitch class. In most compositional situations, decisions about pitch-class values long precede those about the octave positions in which the pitch classes will finally find their incarnations as real tones; this is of course because pitch-class values define harmony, hence structure, hence basic musical meaning; while register only defines contour. But from the standpoint of *hearing*, it is surely true that register (high, low, middle, confined, dispersed, ascending, descending, etc.) impresses itself on the ear more quickly than does pitch-class content. It is true that a trained musician absorbs both together in such quick succession that his apprehension of them is to all intents simultaneous; but the immediacy of registral values is nonetheless obvious.

In register we have our mediator. Registral revisions do "nothing" to affect the basic harmonic relations, while at the same time they can drastically alter phrase shapes, gestural contours, and the like. It is in the realm of registral change, then, that our most powerful remedy for compositional defect may be found. The means and principles for registral revision have already been set forth in the preceding chapter.

Example 50-a shows an instance of a registrally nondescript and deficient line:

EXAMPLE 50–a

Making registral adjustments according to the principles referred to above, example 50-a can be transformed into a line with an improved and varied shape:

EXAMPLE 50–b

Once more, notice the frequent changes of direction in the line, as well as the tendency to express "small" intervals (such as minor and major seconds) as large leaps:

EXAMPLE 51

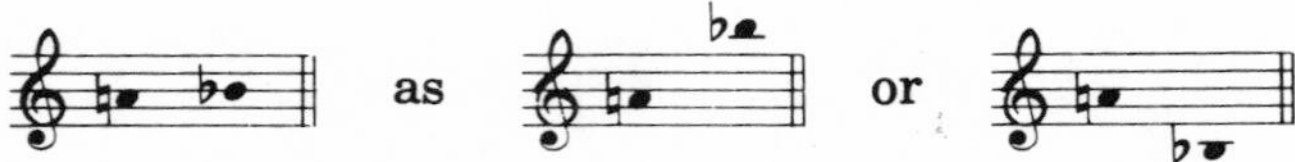

EXERCISES Revise and improve the following passages according to the examples given above. (Keep in mind the nature of the instruments specified for each passage.) Remember that we wish to hear each interval, simultaneous or successive, as clearly as we can; and this is generally easiest when the notes are registrally dispersed. Therefore, half and whole steps, while not "forbidden," will be less frequent than their larger versions as sevenths and ninths; and even larger intervals will often be desirable as octave compounds. Remember too that a line usually ought to "go somewhere"—either end somewhere new, registrally, or go there and return.
(A possible beginning for each passage's revision is provided in all three exercises below.)

1. Possible revision:

3. Possible revision:

Octaves

In our initial definition of register (page 26) we gave octave position as the more precise of the two meanings of the term. The interval of the octave, separating as it does tones of equivalent function, is intimately involved with registral as well as contrapuntal questions. Therefore, we have postponed examining the issue of octaves until now, because most problems with this interval arise as a result of faulty voice leading which needs corrective treatment.

Ever since Schoenberg's celebrated proscription (later withdrawn) against the use of octaves in 12-tone composition, there has hovered a cloud of ambiguity about the proper employment in chromatic music of this simplest of intervals. My belief is that in general the octave should be regarded here somewhat the same way that functional dissonance was regarded in simple diatonic music—that is, as a special intervallic situation, not normal, hence dramatic, and therefore requiring special preparation and treatment. (This situation occurs in chapter 8, example 73, discussed on page 107.) We might enumerate three principle situations in which its use may be considered fruitful:

1. *in a situation requiring particular emphasis on a given pitch class.* The constituent notes of the octave giving emphasis to the chosen pitch either may simply be a doubling of what was originally just a single instance of the note or, more reasonably, could arise as the result of the presence of the same pitch class in more than one voice—in this case with the duplication expressed in different octave positions.

2. *as a "real" interval, rather than a doubling.* Here the most successful intervallic situation for such a use will be one in which the octave is the axial point in an intervallically symmetrical situation. (Example 52 shows several of these, from the simplest to variously arpeggiated and elaborated versions.)

EXAMPLES 52a–d

(a) → or → or

or etc.

(b) → or → or etc.

(c) → → etc.

(d) → etc.

3. *as an "acoustic" doubling, mostly to reinforce low-register tones* (especially with instruments weak in low register, such as the harp). This usage merely continues the traditional practice of reinforcing bass tones, although now the notes themselves no longer have the harmonic function they did in tonal music. Less frequently, one might also double upper-register notes, again as in older music. But in either case, the reinforcing nature of the doubling is made clear by the fact that the doubled notes are at one registral extreme or the other, so that there is no tone from another voice intervening between the main pitch and its octave duplication. Inner-register octave doubling, with its resulting mess of interferences, is to be avoided.

Duration

If you decide that your need for revision extends to problems of rhythmic expression, you must exercise more caution. This is because changes in the durations of individual tones (not, I emphasize, changes of attack point location) can go farther to alter the basic harmonic meaning of a passage than can changes of register, for the shortening of a tone's duration may remove it from some harmonic situation where it contributes a special meaning, and the prolongation of a tone may cause it to persist into a new harmonic situation where its presence alters the previous context. Therefore, these changes, though far less obvious in the immediate surface of the music than are registral revisions, must be considered more fundamental than the latter. That is why we suggest resorting to durational revision only after registral revision has been exhausted as a remedy.

EXAMPLE 53–a

Example 53-a, while not actually annoying, could still be better expressed if the tones of the minor seconds overlapped—thus making the interval seem more purposive in the unfolding of the passage. This we accomplish by the changes shown in example 53-b:

EXAMPLE 53–b

Note the other changes too. Notice, for instance, that in the last measure, prolonging the G-sharp makes the G-sharp/G-natural into a new line, now accompanied by the C-sharp (rather than, as originally, a single line of three pitches), thus relating this measure to the previously occurring overlapped minor seconds.

EXERCISE Revise the following passage by altering the durations of individual tones (shortening them, or prolonging them so that they overlap new attacks). Do *not* alter the time intervals *between* attacks. (See examples 53-a and 53-b for reference.)

Questions (a) Can you see any relation between the tones in the first four measures and those in the last four? (b) Between the same two groups of attack points?

Other Considerations

Compared to registral and durational revision, other possibilities have much less significance, and belong largely to the third general category of revision, to which we referred at the beginning of this chapter. Nevertheless, articulation, dynamics, and—especially—instrumentation of course have a powerful effect on the sense projected by the music. But these belong mainly to later, more cosmetic stages of composing, and the application of changes in these domains is usually governed by far more local and intuitive considerations than the ones we have given here. For although the implementation of registral or durational changes usually comes in response to local circumstances, the principles by which such changes are carried out are independent of the specific situation that calls for them. The same cannot be said of articulative revisions, and it is therefore not practical to try to formulate general principles of "correctness" in this domain.

A final caution: It is only as a last resort that actual changes of pitch class should be contemplated; and the same is nearly as true for attack points, although with the latter there is a bit more flexibility, owing to the fact that time relations are not as precisely received in the ear/mind as is pitch class information. When one takes the scalpel to these parts of the body musical, one runs the risk of fatal amputations. But at the same time, bear in mind that it is the *piece* being written that has the claim, not the *method* by which it was composed. Violation of methodical principles is therefore certainly available to us, and *in extremis* may be necessary. Notice how crucial the attitude here is: We are not talking about ignoring the dictates of whatever method we are employing to write the piece. Rather, we are asserting that the method has brought our composition out of vagueness and obscurity to a certain stage of definition, but that now our *direct* perception of the entity which that composition has become demands the change of this particular note, that attack point, etc. And, above all, because we have tried other less drastic remedies first, we can be comfortable that we have not arbitrarily violated the aids to composing which we ourselves first freely chose at the outset of our endeavor.

EXERCISES

Repair the following passage by changing certain tones. Eliminate the simultaneous and successive octaves. Pick substitute tones that will fill out the total chromatic in each of the first two bars—thus eliminating any pitch class duplications within each measure.

PART III
Structure

CHAPTER SEVEN

The 12-Tone Pitch System: Elements and Operations

Numerical Notation

As we have noted before, our letter names for notes are actually pitch-class names: "G-sharp," for example, does not by itself denote any particular G-sharp, but rather the class of all G-sharps (see page 26). We have also learned that a 12-tone set is an ordered succession of pitch classes rather than specific tones, and that its members achieve specificity only when actually used in a concrete musical situation. When we write down 12-tone sets and other pitch-class successions for purposes of compositional reference, however, we often represent them as note heads on staves, as if they were actual tones. To avoid confusion, and to keep in mind the degree of generality represented by pitch-class successions (as well as to facilitate transformations of and operations on them), it would therefore be helpful to have a more neutral way of notating pitch classes and the relations among them. *Numerical notation* is such a way.

In this system of representation, the twelve pitch classes are numbered sequentially by the integers 0 through 11. If we take A-natural as the starting point, the series A-natural, A-sharp, B-natural, C-natural, C-sharp (or D-flat) . . . will then be represented as 0, 1, 2, 3, 4 . . . What advantage is there in this? A twofold one: First, the neutrality of numbering reminds us that we are dealing not with notes and tunes, but with fundamental relational networks, which we will later express compositionally in myriad ways. Second, each pitch class number carries precise quantitative intervallic information: Pitch class 0 is the note selected as the "origin," pitch class 1 is one semitone above it, 2 is two semitones above it, and so forth. In this way, intervals are precisely measured in the very designations of the pitch classes themselves—thus eliminating the use of a single term ("fifths," for example) to describe intervals of different sizes (diminished fifths, perfect fifths, augmented fifths). By the use of pitch class numbers, intervals are denoted by purely quantitative expressions; they are demystified, stripped of metaphysical (or functionally determined) attributes such as "perfection," "imperfection," "consonance," "dissonance," etc.

But most important, as we shall see shortly, numerical notation allows us to define the basic operations and transformations of the 12-tone system in a precise and objective way. And the advantage to *this* is that once these operations and transformations have been stripped of excess prescriptive baggage (e.g. diatonic "functional" nomenclature), they are left free to be employed by each composer exactly as he wishes.

The system of numerical notation, including certain conventions of usage, may be summarized by the six principles given below:

1. The twelve pitch classes are designated by the integers 0 through 11, sequentially numbered in ascending order.
2. The pitch class assigned as 0 is variable; it may be any of the twelve. Which one it is in a given instance will probably be determined by criteria of order; usually the first pitch class of a 12-tone set will be 0. (Some people like to use a fixed numbering system, with C-natural always 0. This has the advantage of standardization, and is useful in translating pitches into various user languages in computer applications. But when the first pitch class of a set is not C-natural, using fixed numbering obscures the relations among its different forms. Therefore we do not use fixed numbering here.)

Here is a 12-tone set written in both note heads and numbers:

EXAMPLE 54

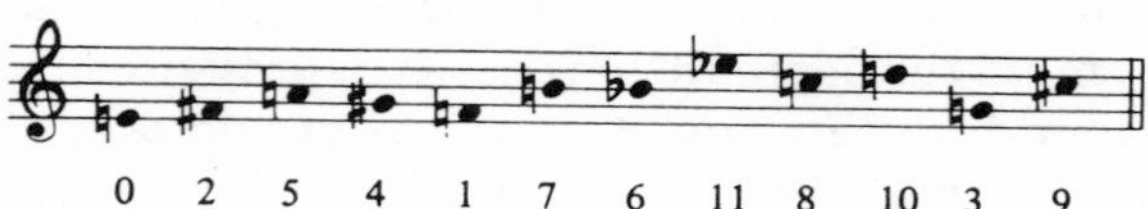

is a particular ordering of

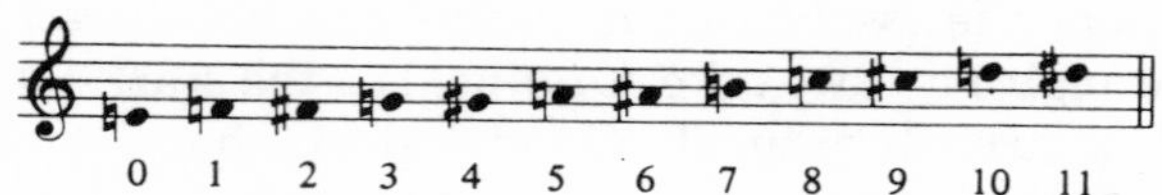

3. There are only twelve distinct pitch classes, and therefore there are only twelve pitch class numbers. If, say, B-flat is pitch class 0, then all B-flats and A-sharps are 0, all C-sharps and D-flats are 3, etc:

EXAMPLE 55

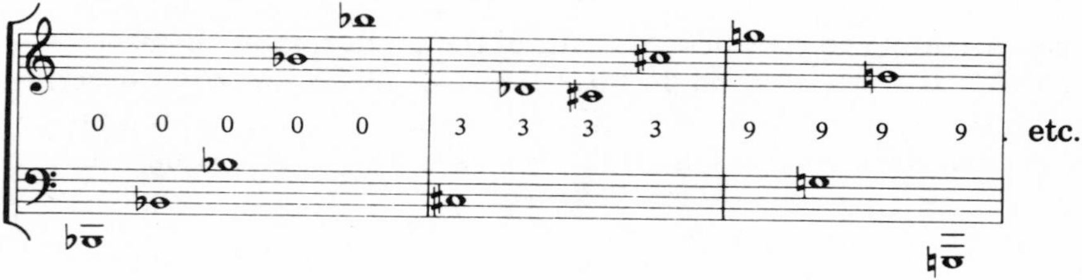

Example 55 shows that all octave-related notes are represented by the same pitch class number.

> **4.** *Intervals* are denoted by quantities, measured in semitones. Thus, for instance, the interval from pitch class 0 to pitch class 4 is 4 semitones (in traditional nomenclature, a "major third"); from 1 to 8 is a 7 ("perfect fifth"), etc.

Example 56 shows a few intervals measured in semitones:

EXAMPLE 56

Now, what of the octave? It is an interval of twelve semitones; it is also the interval between a pitch class and itself—in other words:

> **5.** The interval 12 is equivalent to the interval 0. This is merely an arithmetical way of saying that in pitch class relations, *register* (octave position) plays no part.

Another way of asserting the equivalence of intervals 12 and 0 is to observe that 12 is the *modulus* of the system. It is the interval within each of which the same intervallic pattern of twelve equal semitones is repeated:

EXAMPLE 57

12 semitones = an octave

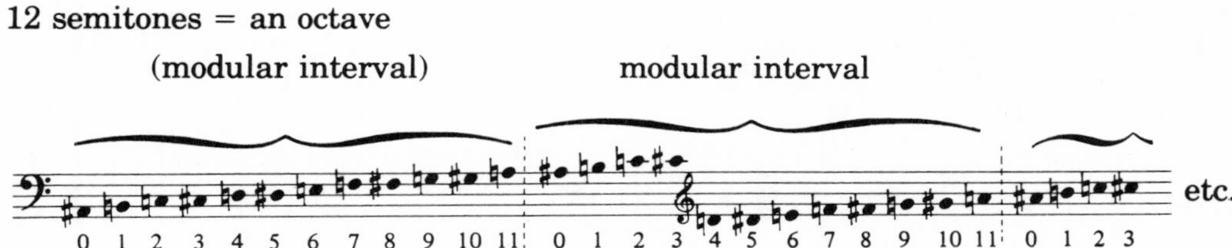

> **6.** Since register plays no part in this labeling system, intervallic *direction* has no real meaning at this stage of our proceedings. This is a property of real notes and intervals, not of pitch classes or interval classes. For this reason, we neither speak of nor represent intervals as "ascending" or "descending." Instead we observe the convention that all intervals are always measured *upwards* from 0. Thus, if C-natural is 0, the "descending" interval C-natural to B-natural is actually between 0 and 11—it is an 11, not a 1.

Example 58 shows various distributions of pitch classes 0 and 11, which involve only the two interval classes 11 and 1:

EXAMPLE 58

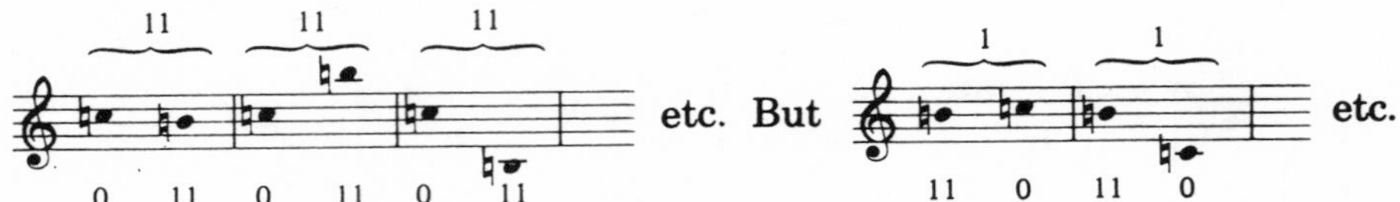

Remember that in all the foregoing discussion, we have really been speaking of interval classes. Therefore, references to an interval class includes within it all the possible octave compounds of an interval class, as well as its most basic, smallest form. In example 59, various specific representations of interval class 7 are shown:

EXAMPLE 59

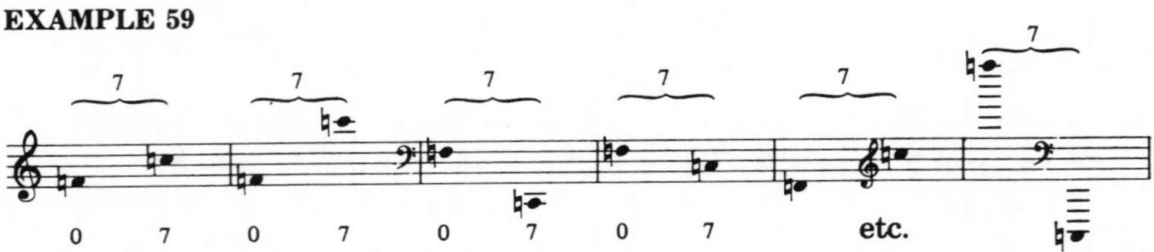

EXERCISES

A. Translate the following into pitch class numbers. Set the first note in exercises 1 and 2 equal to 0; let C-natural = 0 in exercise 3, and D-natural = 0 in exercise 4:

1. 

2. 

3. 

(For simultaneities, write both pitch class numbers one above the other.)

Question Examining the number sequences you have derived for (1) and (2), above, can you see a relation between the two?

B. Translate the following sequences of pitch class numbers into note heads, selecting your own registers. (For the first three sequences, select your own pitch class 0.)

(1) 0 11 2 1 10 8 7 9 3 5 6 4

(2) 0 1 10 11 2 4 5 3 9 7 6 8

(3) 0 7 11 0 7 9 11 0 0 0 11 2 0 7
5

(4) Let A-natural = 0. Express the vertically aligned pitch class numbers as simultaneities, and the dashes as prolongations of the pitch preceding each dash.

Voice I: 0 1——— 10——— 11 2 4 5 3— 9 7——6 8

Voice II: 5 4 7 6 3 1———0— 2 8 10 11 9

Operations

Ever since the initial development of the 12-tone system by Schoenberg, there have been certain fundamental transformations to which 12-tone sets are routinely subjected. (These have in more recent years been supplemented by new ones, some of which we shall consider in chapter 8.)

The operations themselves, while originally designed for application to whole sets, are in fact of course applicable to any collection of pitch classes; in 12-tone music, their use with discrete segments of sets is especially common. (Here once more, we want to remind the reader that these fundamental transformations are on pitch classes, not specific notes.)

The basic operations are:

transposition
inversion
retrogression

When appropriately combined, these transformations yield a group or array of set-forms all of which are closely related to the original set. For this reason (as well as for other more formal ones) the results of these operations are considered to form a group of set-forms whose members are all direct manifestations of the original order.

Transposition, in its traditional meaning, signifies the restating of a line, chord, etc., at some new pitch level; internal intervallic content is usually preserved, but so also is the linear contour and other specifics of the entity being transposed. Example 60 shows a simple instance of diatonic transposition:

EXAMPLE 60

In the 12-tone system, the traditional contour-preserving definition does not necessarily apply; the process is now generalized, signifying an operation on pitch classes. Transposition is here defined as the addition of an interval class of constant size to the original pitch classes. Intervallic content is preserved, independent of register or contour. Now here first appears the operational advantage of numerical notation: Using it, transposition becomes simply the addition of a constant (a number from 0 to 11 representing an interval class of a certain number of semitones) to the pitch classes of the material to be transposed. In example 61, four pitch classes are transposed in this way. Each pitch class in this example has had 6 added to it. The 6 represents 6 semitones, the interval of a tritone:

EXAMPLE 61

Since we have only twelve distinct pitch classes, the transposition operation (like the others to be discussed) can never add any new pitch classes to a complete 12-tone set. (This is in sharp contrast to tonal transposition, in which the main point is often precisely such an addition. A transposition may employ tones not present at all in the original key; this is what modulation from one key to another does, for instance.) Since both the original and the transposed versions of a set contain all twelve pitch classes, we might therefore consider transposition an operation that permutes, that is, *reorders* the elements of the original set. But the essential point to remember is that transposition of a pitch class by an interval class is an operation *modulo* 12 (with respect to a modulus of 12), so that registral values have no place in this fundamental definition. (Indeed, this idea is not foreign to tonal music either, for when we talk of a theme transposed from tonic to dominant, we mean a transposition of pitch class content, not caring whether the dominant is expressed, say, at the upper fifth or the lower fourth.) Thus, if we transpose 0 by 7, 7 results. But if we transpose 7 by 7 again, we reach not "pitch class 14" (which doesn't exist), but pitch class 2, which is 14 (*mod* 12), or 14 minus 12. (Remember that interval class 12, the octave, is equivalent to interval class 0.) Example 62 summarizes the foregoing:

EXAMPLE 62

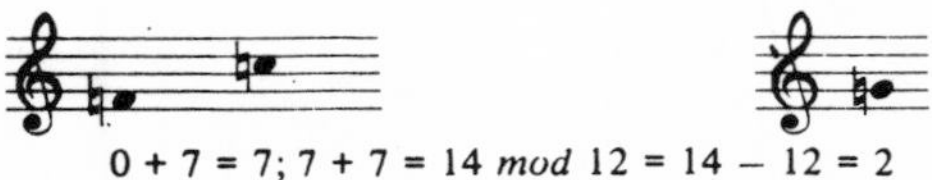

More concisely, $T_7(0) = 7$; $T_7(7) = 2$.

From the preceding discussion, it is clear that there can be only twelve distinct transposition levels (T-levels), one corresponding to each pitch class. Example 63 (to be completed by the reader) shows the twelve transpositions of a 12-tone set:

EXAMPLE 63 The 12 T's of a set.

(N.B. 11 + 1 = 12 *mod* 12 = 0)

EXERCISE: Fill in the remaining T's between T_3 and T_{11}, using note heads and pitch class numbers

Inversion in diatonic music traditionally means either (1) reversing the contour direction of a line (what went up in the original now goes down, and vice versa), usually adhering to the dictates of the given key rather than maintaining the line's exact intervals in its upside-down expression; or (2) permuting the registral order of tones in chords (e.g., changing the root position of a triad to its "first inversion" by moving the root up an octave and leaving the third as the lowest tone)—which is really octave transposing. But in the 12-tone system, the definition has been generalized so as to make it independent of register, direction, and other properties of actual notes, and once again it is couched purely in terms of relations among pitch classes. Like transposition, this operation can conveniently be described as an arithmetic operation on pitch class numbers, as follows:

The inversion of a pitch or interval class is its complement *mod* 12—that is, it is the *difference* between the original quantity and 12. If the letter "I" represents the operation of *inversion,* then:

I(pitch class) = 12 − pitch class

Thus, the inversion of pitch or interval class

1 is 11
2 is 10
3 is 9
4 is 8
5 is 7
6 is 6

and vice versa; the table may be read in both directions. Thus, the inversion of pitch or interval class

7 is 5
8 is 4
9 is 3
10 is 2
11 is 1

Notice also that 12, like 6, is its own complement (12 − 0 = 12 = 0). An interval and its complement always add up to 12, or 0 *modulo* 12.

Example 64-a shows inversion starting with pitch class 0; for this reason, the I-form will itself start on 0.

EXAMPLE 64–a

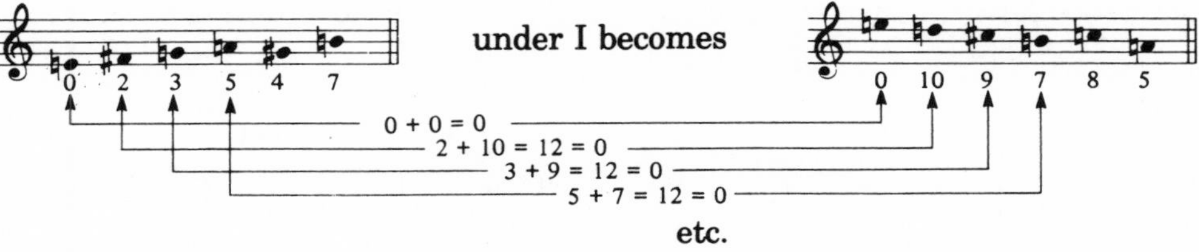

The sum of an interval and its complement, *mod* 12, is always 0.

Example 64-b shows the inversion of another pitch-class succession, this time starting on a pitch class other than 0; here, the I-form will begin with the complement of the initial pitch class of this example.

EXAMPLE 64–b

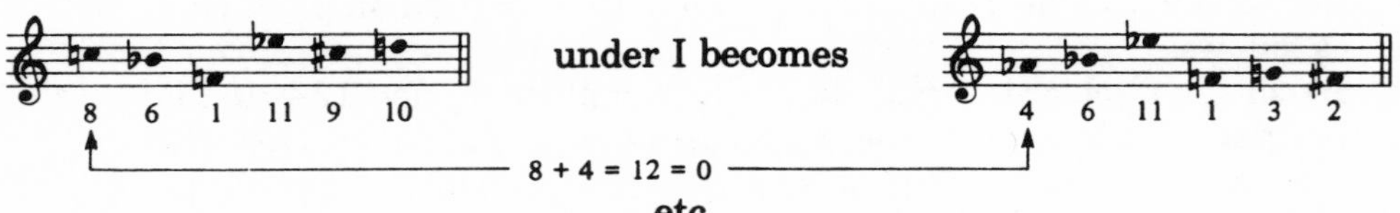

etc.

From the above discussion, it should be clear that inversion can be defined exclusively as a numerical operation, just as we saw transposition could be; in this case, the operation is complementation *mod* 12 of the pitch class numbers—arithmetically, 12 minus each pitch class number.

Retrogression in the traditional diatonic sense means the reversal of the order of occurrence of a series of events. This meaning is preserved in the 12-tone system, and since a 12-tone or other ordered set is an ordered succession of pitch classes, its retrograde (denoted by the letter "R") is simply the original strand of elements now presented in reverse order. Example 65-a shows a 12-tone set and its retrograde:

EXAMPLE 65–a

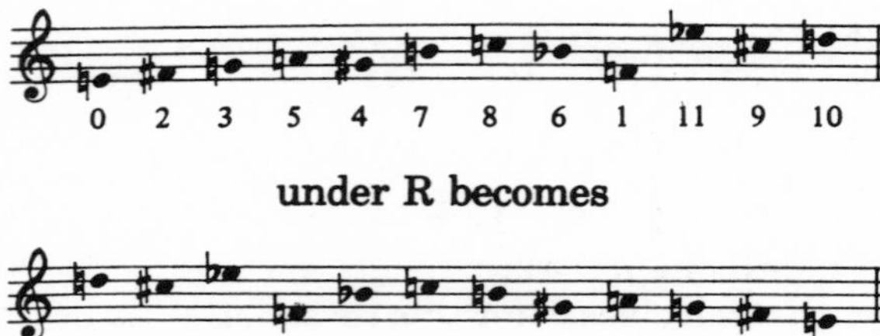

Example 65-b shows a rhythmic succession, here diatonic, with its retrograde. Notice that not only is the order of notes reversed, but that also the time intervals between adjacent elements are similarly presented in reverse order.

EXAMPLE 65–b

There is actually a way of regarding retrogression as a numerical operation like T (transposition) and I (inversion), but this involves representing pitch classes by pairs of numbers, one of which is the pitch class number we have already encountered, and the other a number denoting order position. Then, retrogression is defined as the complementation of order numbers, just as inversion is defined as the complementation of pitch class numbers. However, though this is of great theoretical and conceptual importance, it is a formal rather than a practical definition and need not concern us further here.

The three fundamental operations may be combined to make composite transformations, and the following discussion will include a few examples of this. In particular, it is usual to combine inversion and retrogression into *retrograde-inversion* (abbreviated "RI," and itself considered a fundamental operation) and also to regard transposition (T) as somewhat separate from the collection of transformations represented by the four symbols S (standing for the original set; often also called "O" for original or "P" for prime), R, I, and RI. These four transformations are regarded as the four basic forms of the set.

In example 66-a we see the set S_0 from example 63 transposed by 7 semitones and retrograded (denoted by R_7).

EXAMPLE 66–a

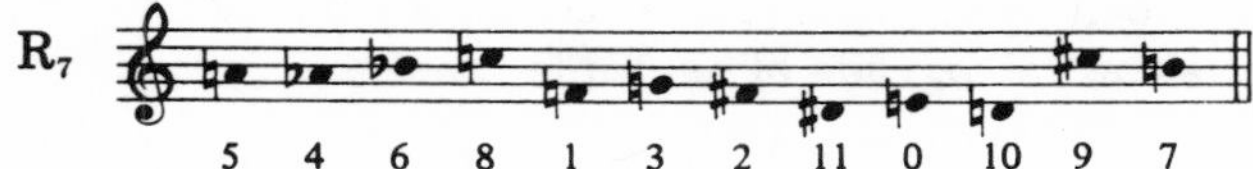

Notice here that it is the *last* element which is 7, defining the transpositional level. This is because we are dealing here with a retrograde, in which the last element corresponds to the *first* element of the original S. Unless we do this, the retrograde of this R (which will yield an S-form) will not be at the same transpositional level as the original S_7. Always reckon transposition levels in R- or RI- forms by the *last* rather than the *first* element.

Here we must warn the reader that our labeling of R- and RI-forms is not the standard one, in which transposition levels are reckoned by the first element. The general practice is, from a formal and theoretical point of view, more consistent than ours, and the theoretical and analytic literature therefore usually follows it. But in this book, we are not theorists, we are composers. And whatever formal reasons there may be for this labeling must give way to procedural ease in the *use* of these forms. When you are composing with 12-tone sets, it is much more convenient to have them labeled in such a way that retrogrades of the same pitch succession show the same T-number, even though it does not conform to theoretical consistency.

Example 66-b shows the set S_0 of example 63 inverted without transposition (denoted by I_0):

EXAMPLE 66–b

Example 66-c shows the above I-form now transposed by 3 (denoted by I_3):

EXAMPLE 66–c

Notice here that in combination with inversion, transposition is applied *after* the operation of inversion. This procedure guarantees that the I-form will have as its first element the pitch class corresponding to its transposition level—because I(0) is 0 (read: the inversion of zero is zero), plus the T-value gives I(T-value). In the above example if we had transposed first, the first stage of the process of transformation would have yielded S_3; and when inverted, its first element—3—would have become 9. We would then have the peculiar situation of something called I_3 beginning not with pitch class 3 but with 9.

Finally, example 66-d shows the retrograde of example 66-c:

EXAMPLE 66–d

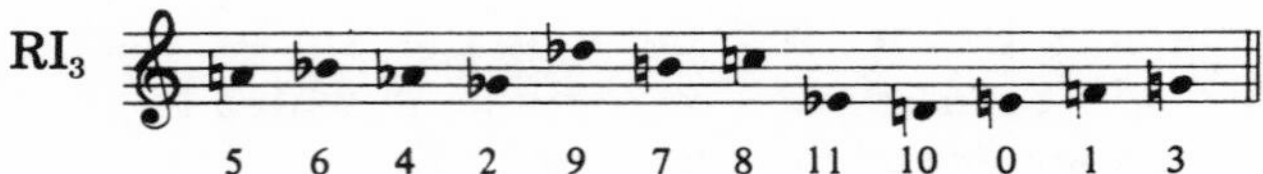

Observe that here, as with the R-form in example 66-a, the T-level is given by the last, not the first, element.

EXERCISE Transform the set S_0 of example 63 into the following forms, writing out the results both in note heads and pitch class numbers:

(a) S_7 (b) R_8 (c) I_2 (d) RI_6 (e) R_6 (f) I_{10} (g) R_9 (h) S_3
(i) RI_{11} (j) RI_0 (k) S_0 (l) I_0

With the three operations we have described—transposition, inversion, and retrogression—and their combinations, we are equipped to form the traditional basic array of transformations of a 12-tone set that were first put forth by Schoenberg. Now let us exclude T for a moment; denoting the original set by S we find that, using the operations of inversion and retrogression, there can only exist four possible transformations of S, including S itself. They are:

S, RI, R, and I

Example 67 shows a set, furnished with its four basic forms:

EXAMPLE 67

If S_0 is

then RI_0 is

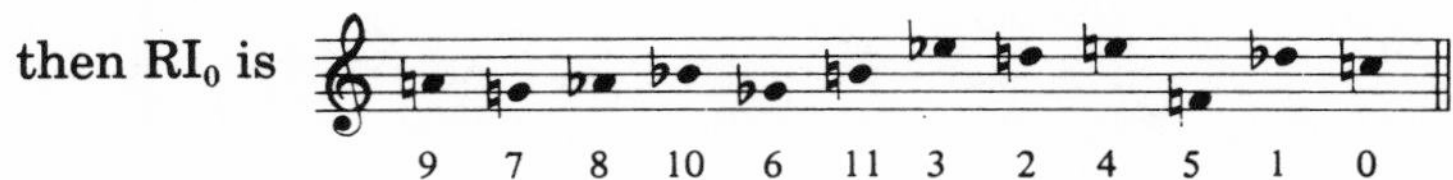

and R_0 is

and I_0 is

Notice that any one of these forms can be produced as a transformation of any of the others by an appropriate operation or combination of operations. Thus,

RI is:	RI of S	R is:	R of S	I is:	I of S
	R of I		RI of I		RI of R
	I of R		I of RI		R of RI

Moreover, of course, S is R of R, I of I, and RI of RI.

EXERCISES

1. Verify the above equivalences by applying the operations given above to the indicated set-forms from example 67. Write your results in note heads and pitch class numbers, and label the set-forms.
2. When these four basic forms are combined with their twelve possible T-levels, a total of 12 × 4 (or 48) forms result. The following portion of a table begins to present the T-levels for the four basic forms of the set from example 67. Fill in the note heads that are missing above their corresponding pitch class numbers:

3. Continue and complete the above table, writing out T_3 through T_{11} for each of the four forms, both in note heads and pitch class numbers. Make sure to check your work for any duplication of pitches within a set; if there are any, you have made an error.

We have now produced the forty-eight traditional forms of a single 12-tone set that were introduced by Schoenberg. Here we should remark that no matter what combination of the operations of R, I, RI, or T you may apply, you will never generate anything other than one of these forty-eight forms. To begin, since T is an operation *mod* 12, there being therefore only twelve distinct transposition levels, only one of these twelve levels will ever be produced by any interval of transposition, no matter what it is. Thus, T_1 of T_9, which we may notate as $T_1(T_9) = T_{10}$; $T_1(T_{11}) = T_0$; $T_{11}(T_2) = T_1$; $T_3(T_{10}) = T_1$; etc., etc.

Furthermore, as we have just hinted, applying any one of the basic operations S (the identity operation), RI, R, or I to any one of the four basic forms will only result in another of the four. So, for instance, under the operation of inversion, denoted as I:

S yields I
R yields RI
I yields S
RI yields R

and the reader can easily verify similar results starting with any of the other three basic forms. These properties are usually summarized in an array like this:

S	RI	R	I
RI	S	I	R
R	I	S	RI
I	R	RI	S

The meaning of the array can be explained by regarding, say, all the rows in it as set-forms, and all the columns as operations. (It can be equally well done reversing rows and columns.) Then if we regard, say, the top row in the table as forms, and the left-hand columns as operations, the intersection of a row and a column gives the result of applying the operation in the left-hand position of that row (i.e., from the column on the left) to the set-form at the head of the column (i.e., in the top row of the table). Thus, for instance, reading down the second column, under RI, shows:

RI(RI) = S,
R(RI) = I
I(RI) = R

Notice how the main diagonals in this arrangement are formed by S and I, and how S(S) = S = RI(RI), R(R), and I(I). And finally, notice that the particular order of the top row and the left-hand column is arbitrary; we could arrange these sequences in any of the twenty-four orders available with four elements and the result would be similar to the ones we have achieved above.

From all this it should be clear that these various operations and their results form a closed system of transformations. For this reason, we have formulated a convenient way of summarizing all forty-eight basic forms in a 12 × 12 array of pitch class numbers. In example 68, the forty-eight forms of the set from example 67 have been arranged as follows:

EXAMPLE 68 A 12 × 12 array.

transpositions of S arranged in I-order

	I_0	I_{11}	I_7	I_8	I_{10}	I_9	I_1	I_6	I_2	I_4	I_5	I_3	
S_0	0	11	7	8	10	9	1	6	2	4	5	3	R_0
S_1	1	0	8	9	11	10	2	7	3	5	6	4	R_1
S_5	5	4	0	1	3	2	6	11	7	9	10	8	R_5
S_4	4	3	11	0	2	1	5	10	6	8	9	7	R_4
S_2	2	1	9	10	0	11	3	8	4	6	7	5	R_2
S_3	3	2	10	11	1	0	4	9	5	7	8	6	R_3
S_{11}	11	10	6	7	9	8	0	5	1	3	4	2	R_{11}
S_6	6	5	1	2	4	3	7	0	8	10	11	9	R_6
S_{10}	10	9	5	6	8	7	11	4	0	2	3	1	R_{10}
S_8	8	7	3	4	6	5	9	2	10	0	1	11	R_8
S_7	7	6	2	3	5	4	8	1	9	11	0	10	R_7
S_9	9	8	4	5	7	6	10	3	11	1	2	0	R_9
	RI_0	RI_{11}	RI_7	RI_8	RI_{10}	RI_9	RI_1	RI_6	RI_2	RI_4	RI_5	RI_3	

Here we see the twelve transpositions of S, written one under the other in successive rows, using pitch class numbers only. The order of their arrangement, however, is the same as that of the *pitch classes* of the I-form starting on 0. This simple arrangement condenses the forty-eight forms into the neat array above, with which we can read off any transposition of S by finding the pitch class corresponding to the T-level on which we wish to start and simply reading the rows from left to right; likewise, we can find any T of R by reading the rows from right to left, any T of I by reading the columns down, and any T of RI by reading the columns up. Furthermore, we can read off information about the *interval* succession of the set by examining the diagonals of the array. Thus, the main top-left to bottom-right diagonal (all the 0's) gives the interval between each pitch class in the set and itself—that is, of course, zero. The next diagonal immediately to the right gives the interval between adjacent pitch classes, i.e., the interval succession of the set. The next gives the interval between pitch classes *two* order positions apart, and so forth. All forty-eight forms are labeled, with arrows showing the direction in which the succession is to be read for each form.

Such a concise formation has an advantage beyond mere efficiency; it also serves to impress on its user how closely interrelated these forty-eight forms really are. In all of them, the interval succession is virtually unchanged; the most that ever happens to it is that it may be reversed (under RI), or complemented (under I), or both (under R). The interval succession is totally unaffected by transposition.

Parenthetically, let us observe that RI, the one composite of the four basic forms, is actually more closely related to S than are I or R. The reason lies in the fact that when an interval is retrograded, it changes to its complement:

1. from 4 to 8 is a 4, = 4 (4 8), but from 8 to 4 is an 8, = 8 (8 4)

2. from 0 to 1 is a 1, = 1 (0 1), but from 1 to 0 is an 11, = 11 (1 0)

Therefore, the intervals of R are *reversed complements* of those of S. But RI, being the I of R, complements the complements, thus leaving its interval succession merely the reverse of that of S:

3. from 0 to 2 is a 2; its R is therefore a 10, while the I of the 10, which is therefore the RI of the original 2, is now again itself a 2.

EXERCISES

1. Write out in note heads, with the corresponding pitch class numbers beneath them, the array of example 68. Since there are twelve transpositions of S, you will need twelve staves. Make sure to align vertically the note heads in each column.
2. Write out in note heads, with the corresponding pitch class numbers beneath them, the following forms from the array of example 68:

   (a) S_0 (b) RI_3 (c) I_7 (d) R_9 (e) R_6

   (f) RI_4 (g) S_{11} (h) I_8 (i) I_0 (j) RI_0 (k) R_0
3. Make 12×12 arrays (in note heads with pitch class numbers beneath them) from the following:

(a) First fill in the missing pitch class numbers, then make your array.

(b) First fill in the missing note heads, then make your array. Look at the array after you have finished it. The second hexachord of this set is RI_{11} of the first hexachord. How many *distinct* set-forms are there? What is the relation between the pairs of set-forms that are duplicates of each other? Make a table in which you list the set-forms that are identical, in pairs. What does this have to do with the structure of the original S_0?

(c) First take I_7 of the given tetrachord; then follow it with T_8. The three tetrachords together will make a complete 12-tone set. Rearrange, if you like, the order in which the two generated tetrachords follow the original one (but do not change their internal orderings), and then make your array.

CHAPTER EIGHT

The 12-Tone Pitch System: Further Operations

In recent years, certain other operations on the pitch-class successions of 12-tone sets have come into use. We will consider only two, and between them they represent the next level of transformation beyond that of the fundamental operations discussed in chapter 7. One of them transforms the interval *content* of sets (or any other pitch-class succession); it is called *multiplicative transformation* and is represented by the letter M. The other operation transforms the *order* of pitch classes (resulting in "order transposition") and it is called *rotation*. These two classes of operation are not as fundamental to the 12-tone system as T, R, and I; so we will only consider them briefly and add a few remarks on how they might be used in composing music.

Multiplicative Transformation

Multiplicative transformation actually alters certain interval classes in a pitch-class succession. Specifically, all minor seconds (interval class 1) are changed into perfect fifths (interval class 7), and vice versa. This transformation may be defined and explained in several ways:

1. as an arithmetic operation, in which the pitch-class numbers of the original are *multiplied* by 7, *mod* 12 (denoted by M7). This is why the operation is called multiplicative.

EXERCISE Write out the ascending chromatic scale in pitch-class numbers. Now multiply each number by 7, *mod* 12 (i.e., leaving for each multiplication only the remainder after all integral multiples of 12 have been subtracted). What is the result: Translate this result into note heads, with C-natural=0.

2. as a reordering of a pitch-class succession so that instead of being an ordering of the basic ascending succession of pitch class numbers—the "ascending chromatic scale" (0, 1, 2, 3, . . . 10, 11)—it becomes an ordering of the "cycle of fifths" (0, 7, 2, 9, . . . 10, 5). In this interpretation of the transformation, the two orderings are correlated element for element, thus:

Original:	0	1	2	3	4	5	6	7	8	9	10	11
Transformation:	0	7	2	9	4	11	6	1	8	3	10	5

Then, whatever their order of occurrence in the succession being transformed, every element in the original ordering correlates with one in the new ordering.

EXERCISE Write out the above two cycles in note heads, choosing your own 0, and verify that the second is indeed the cycle of fifths. Arrange them on two lines so that corresponding pitch classes are vertically aligned. Notice that half of them are unchanged. What characteristic is shared by the pitch classes that don't change? (It is shown by their pitch class numbers.)

3. as the transposition of all odd-numbered pitch classes by a tritone: 0 is unchanged, 1 under T_6 becomes 7, etc.

EXERCISE Once more write out the ascending chromatic scale. Transpose the odd-numbered pitch classes by a tritone (interval class 6); leave the even-numbered pitch classes unchanged. What is the result?

Thus far, we have given three definitions or recipes for the transformation and have shown its effect on the simplest of possible orderings—the succession 0, 1, 2, 3, . . . 10, 11. Now, in example 69, we apply it to an ordered 12-tone set, displaying the M7-form beneath the original S.

EXAMPLE 69

Once more, notice that all even-numbered pitch classes (0, 2, 4, . . .) are unchanged, and that the odd-numbered ones are all T_6. Notice that every minor second has been changed to a perfect fifth, and vice versa. Here lies the reason why even-numbered pitch classes, which are separated from each other by *major* seconds, remain unchanged: A major second (a 2) is the sum of two minor seconds (1 plus 1); but when minor seconds (1's) are altered to fifths (7's), the major second changes to an interval that is the sum of two fifths (7 plus 7 = 14, *mod* 12 = 2). But what is this interval? A major second once again.

Let us summarize the pitch-class changes under M7 in this table:

0 remains 0 = 0, *mod* 12		0 remains 0
1 becomes 7 = 7, *mod* 12		1 becomes 7
2 becomes 14 = 2, *mod* 12		2 remains 2
3 becomes 21 = 9, *mod* 12		3 becomes 9
4 becomes 28 = 4, *mod* 12		4 remains 4
5 becomes 35 = 11, *mod* 12	or	5 becomes 11
6 becomes 42 = 6, *mod* 12		6 remains 6
7 becomes 49 = 1, *mod* 12		7 becomes 1
8 becomes 56 = 8, *mod* 12		8 remains 8
9 becomes 63 = 3, *mod* 12		9 becomes 3
10 becomes 70 = 10, *mod* 12		10 remains 10
11 becomes 77 = 5, *mod* 12		11 becomes 5

The table shows that pairs of values exchange places. For instance, 1 goes to 7 and 7 goes to 1; in any succession transformed by M7, all intervals 1 are changed into intervals 7, and vice versa. The reason why one can describe the transformation as selective transposition by 6 is that 6 (the tritone) is the difference between interval 1 and interval 7. (The other pairs that exchange places are 3 and 9, and 5 and 11.)

From all this, it is clear that M7 is quite close to the fundamental operations of R, I, and T and, like them, may be considered a permutation operation. However, it disarranges the original succession more than they do, for although it holds half of the pitch classes unchanged (the pitch classes 0, 2, 4, 6, 8, and 10), it alters the others—albeit in a consistent way.

Multiplicative transformation also possesses interesting intersections with the basic S/RI/R/I array, as well as its own group of derived transformations, which like the basic array also form a closed group. The inversion of M7—since M7 itself is a mapping of a chromatic-scale ordering onto a cycle-of-fifths ordering—is equivalent to the result of taking the original chromatic-scale ordering and mapping it onto the cycle of *fourths*. For the cycle of fourths (0, 5, 10, 3, . . . 2, 7) is the inversion of the cycle of fifths, just as the descending chromatic scale (0, 11, 10, . . . 1) is the inversion of the ascending. The inversion of M7 is also equivalent to multiplying the original pitch class numbers by 5, *mod* 12, and is therefore denoted by M5. In other words, M7 = I(M5), and vice versa.

These relations are clearly expressed in tabular form:

Original:	0	1	2	3	4	5	6	7	8	9	10	11
M7 transformation:	0	7	2	9	4	11	6	1	8	3	10	5
Inversion:	0	11	10	9	8	7	6	5	4	3	2	1
M5 transformation:	0	5	10	3	8	1	6	11	4	9	2	7

Notice another relation here: while I is normally defined as complementing of pitch class numbers *mod* 12, there is also another way to get it: multiply the pitch class numbers of S by 11, *mod* 12.

EXERCISE Multiply the twelve pitch class numbers by 11, *mod* 12, and write them out. If the original ordering is 0, 1, 2, . . . 11, what is the result?

The original S could also, for the sake of formal nicety, be regarded as the result of multiplying its pitch class numbers by 1; thus, we could label S as "M1" and I as "M11." Then we can make a four-group table just as we did for S, RI, R, and I—but this time involving only multiplicative operations:

M1	M5	M7	M11
M5	M1	M11	M7
M7	M11	M1	M5
M11	M7	M5	M1

(Remember that S = M1 and I = M11.)

This array functions just as the other did: Applying any of the four operations to any of the four forms will never yield anything other than another of the four forms. Thus, this group too is closed, with two of its members in common with those of the S/RI/R/I array.

And of course, M7 may be treated independently and furnished with its own 12 × 12 array of the forty-eight fundamental forms.

EXERCISES

1. Take the set of example 69; make a 12 × 12 array, in note heads and pitch-class numbers, of its M7 form.
2. Refer to exercise 3(b) on page 97. Form a 12 × 12 array—in pitch class numbers only—for this set; then transform it under M7, and make a 12 × 12 array of its M7 form. Compare the two arrays. What varies and what is constant between the two?

Rotation

In general, rotation is defined as *order transposition*—that is, instead of changing pitch classes into other pitch classes, we will here change their *position* in the ordered succession of pitch classes. The simplest process for changing the order position of a series of elements is *cyclic permutation,* in which, under successive stages of the transformation, each element in the series advances (or, alternatively, retreats) one position; the element that advances beyond one end of the series moves to the other end. Thus we have a circular process with as many separate and distinct stages in the cycle as there are elements being rotated. Example 70-a shows the rotation of a 12-tone set (but, as you can see, several stages have been left out). Observe how from one stage to the next, each element advances one position to the left, except for the first element, which moves into last place:

EXAMPLE 70–a

EXERCISE Complete rotations 3 through 10 in the blank spaces left in example 70-a. Notice that the twelfth rotation would be the same as the original; that is, rotation 12 = rotation 0.

Clearly, the rotation operation can be applied to segments of any length. For instance, if applied to the successive dyads of a set, it produces a two-stage cycle:

EXAMPLE 70–b

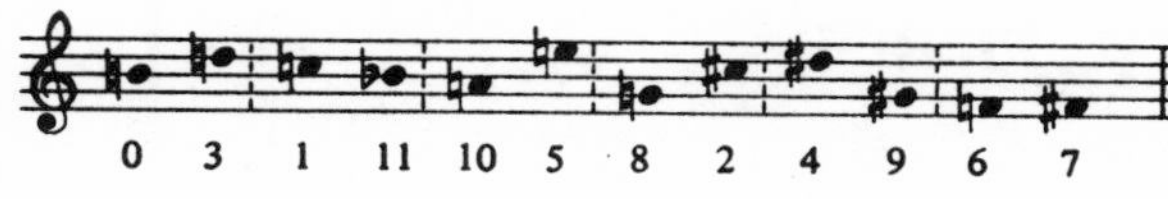

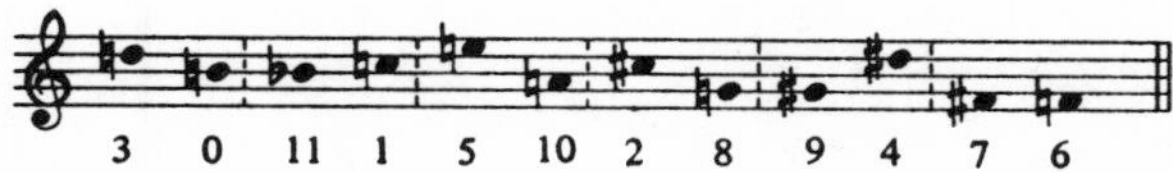

to trichords, a three-stage cycle:

EXAMPLE 70–c

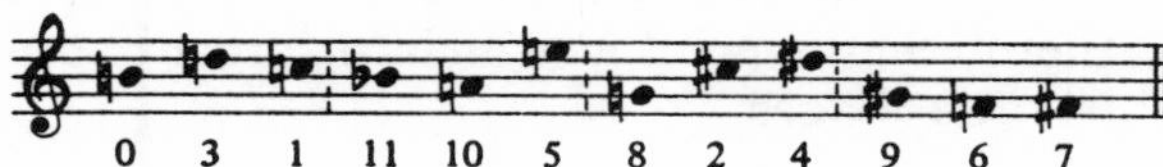

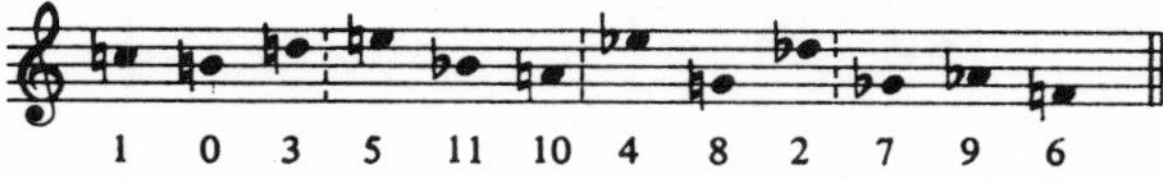

and it will yield a four-stage cycle if applied to tetrachords. However, by far its most general use is as applied to hexachords, for instance:

EXAMPLE 70–d

Of course, any of these segments can be rotated separately, outside of their environments within 12-tone sets.

Rotation of asymmetrical divisions of a set is also possible. Example 70-e displays the beginning of a rotation for a 5/7 division of a 12-tone set. This division produces a 35-stage cycle, since five stages are needed to complete the pentad cycle, while seven are required for the heptad cycle. The least common multiple of these is of course 35; therefore, the point at which the order of the original set is restored is after thirty-five stages.

EXAMPLE 70–e

EXERCISE Complete the remaining stages of this rotation. There will be thirty-five in all.

Here we ought to note a similarity between rotation and multiplicative transformation. Whereas the multiplicatives are the nearest interval-changing transformation to the basic 48-form array by virtue of the controlled and limited alteration they make in the interval *content* of 12-tone sets, the rotation operation is likewise the nearest in the domain of interval *order* change.

If we take the hexachord of example 71-a:

EXAMPLE 71–a

and transform it under M7:

EXAMPLE 71–b

we see that the three intervals marked with an "x" have been changed from the original state. Now if we take the same hexachord of example 71-a and rotate it once:

EXAMPLE 71–c

we see that shifting the first element to the last position adds one new interval (marked with an "x"), but also shifts the other, unaltered intervals each one position to the left. Thus in a rough way, the intervallic disarrangement caused by the two kinds of operation, though different in kind, is similar in degree.

Finally, let us consider one special case of rotation, included because of its importance in the 12-tone works of Stravinsky, as well as with other composers. We illustrate it only for hexachords, as that is its commonest use, but of course it can be applied to strands of any number of elements. This operation is composite; it combines rotation as we have described it with the transposition of each new stage in the cycle, so that every one of them begins on the same pitch class. In example 72 this process is displayed. Compare it with 70-d, part (a), in which the same hexachord is rotated without the transpositions:

EXAMPLE 72

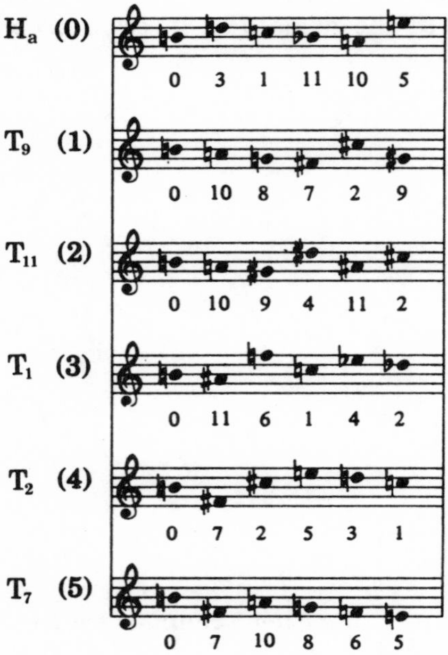

In example 72, each stage of rotation is transposed so that it begins on pitch class 0. What is the result of carrying this rotation-transposition process one stage further?

The closeness of this composite operation to the basic ones can be seen in the fact that the array of example 72:

0	3	1	11	10	5
0	10	8	7	2	9
0	10	9	4	11	2
0	11	6	1	4	2
0	7	2	5	3	1
0	7	10	8	6	5

is actually the result of rotating the elements of each row so that the main diagonal in the standard array (from upper-left to lower-right) becomes the first column in the transformed array:

0	3	1	11	10	5
9	0	10	8	7	2
11	2	0	10	9	4
1	4	2	0	11	6
2	5	3	1	0	7
7	10	8	6	5	0

It is immediately obvious that the pitch class that is repeated from one stage to the next through all five transformations—pitch class 0, or B-natural—appears in the transformed array only in the first order position (i.e., the first column) and nowhere else. This makes it possible to regard the duplicated pitch class as a point of departure (or, under R, a point of arrival) in a compositional situation in which the hexachords are run off simultaneously. In fact, a frequent use of this hexachordal array is to regard elements in the same order position as members of an actual simultaneity, or chord. Using the hexachord transformations of example 72, we demonstrate this practice in example 73:

EXAMPLE 73

Notice several details:

1. The initial B-natural stands for six B-naturals, one contributed by each hexachord.
2. Example 73 is expressed in actual *notes,* that are given registral values, while example 72 is expressed only in pitch classes.
3. The order of rotation-transposition stages from example 72 is preserved registrally in the chords comprising example 73. (They could equally well have been read from the top down.) However, there is no imperative when making these "verticalizations" to preserve the original order of generation in the registral order of the chords;

Point (3) above leads us to another important observation—namely, that the rotation-transposition process with most hexachords will generate occasional pitch class duplications in similar order positions and therefore in chords extracted from them; this although there are in fact a few hexachords which avoid such duplications. If, as in example 73, we preserve the generating order registrally, octaves will inevitably result in the verticals. It would seem here that the process of generation makes these octaves intervallically acceptable, and this is one of the rare cases within the chromatic universe in which octaves actually have an intervallic, as opposed to a duplicating, role.

Finally, note that these verticals may be arpeggiated, that is, linearized, to make tunes that are only distantly related to the original hexachordal material. And furthermore, the whole hexachordal array can of course be subjected to any of the other 12-tone operations we have previously described, in any combination. Examples 74-a and 74-b show two such transformations:

EXAMPLE 74

EXERCISES

1. Complete the transcription of examples 74-a and 74-b into pitch class numbers. This has already been done for the first two verticals in each example.
2. The following is a linearization (or arpeggiation) of example 74-a; each vertical has been rearranged into a linear succession. Compare this with the linear characteristics of the original hexachord and its rotation-transpositions.

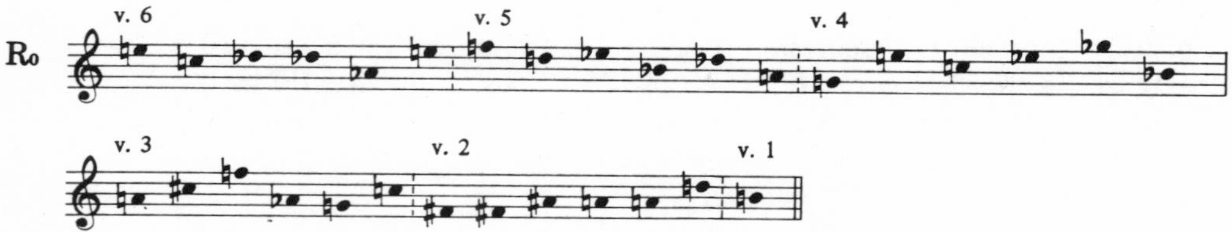

3. Write out a linearization of example 74-b the same way it has been done in exercise 2 for example 74-a. (Read from the bottom up.)
4. Make actual melodies (specifying all rhythmic, dynamic, etc., detail) out of the linearization given in exercise 2, above, and out of your own linearization in exercise 3.

5. Make an array of verticals out of hexachord 1(b) in example 70-d (page 104).

Remarks

We have been describing formal operations and properties of the 12-tone system, and we shall continue this in the next chapters. But we should make the point before proceeding that all these relations are "objective"—that is, they have predictable results based on the consistency and simplicity of their definitions, and the materials (pitch classes) which they transform. But there is nothing prescriptive about them. Composers have found them useful as means of transforming and extending basic pitch material, and of generating much out of little (which is ever the way toward great art) by simple means. However, it cannot be too strongly stated that the objective existence of the relations we have described entails no obligation actually to *use* them. And moreover, their mere use guarantees nothing. They only provide a framework and a support for artistic choice. Here I wish to remind you of the notion, first presented on page 13, of the process-chain of composition. The operations already described, and the systematic methods to be outlined below, provide only minimum conditions for composing when they are employed. They do not really constitute the act of composing itself; but they may be necessary as the means by which a musician can define for himself the universe of musical relations *within which* he will compose his piece. He must not mistake the carrying out of these processes for the piece itself. It is a common fault in 12-tone music, much to be guarded against, that this confusion takes place. Pieces like this give the impression of buildings whose skeletons are in place, but whose walls—let alone whose pleasing details—have been forgotten.

There is another point we should like to make before proceeding, with regard to the idea of *number*. We have gone to the trouble of defining every operation we have discussed in arithmetic terms, and have introduced numerical representation of pitch classes. This situation immediately leads us to realize that since we have really been operating on the numbers rather than the actual pitch classes themselves, we might equally well decide to have these numbers stand for something other than pitch classes—indeed, for anything we please. This is the secret of transferring the organizing power of 12-tone operations (which all have their origins in pitch relations) to other musical domains—most importantly to the flow of musical time. How this is done we shall examine later on, but for the moment it suffices to point out again the enormous value inherent in a powerful generalization. As long as we think of these operations as transformations of actual tones, our imagination will never allow us successfully to transfer the relations they embody to other areas. (This failure, by the way, seems the reason for the collapse of European serial music of the 1950s.) But when we have a neutral and correct way of describing our operations (numerical notation, *mod* 12), the power of substitution can propel them, and us, into any area we wish.

Finally, it may be useful to place the operations, arrays, and elements of this chapter in a coherent diagrammatic perspective that allows us to see how much flowers from a single root. In writing a piece of music using these constructs, we recommend arranging their transformations in an order similar to that proposed in this diagram, for the sake of visual clarity:

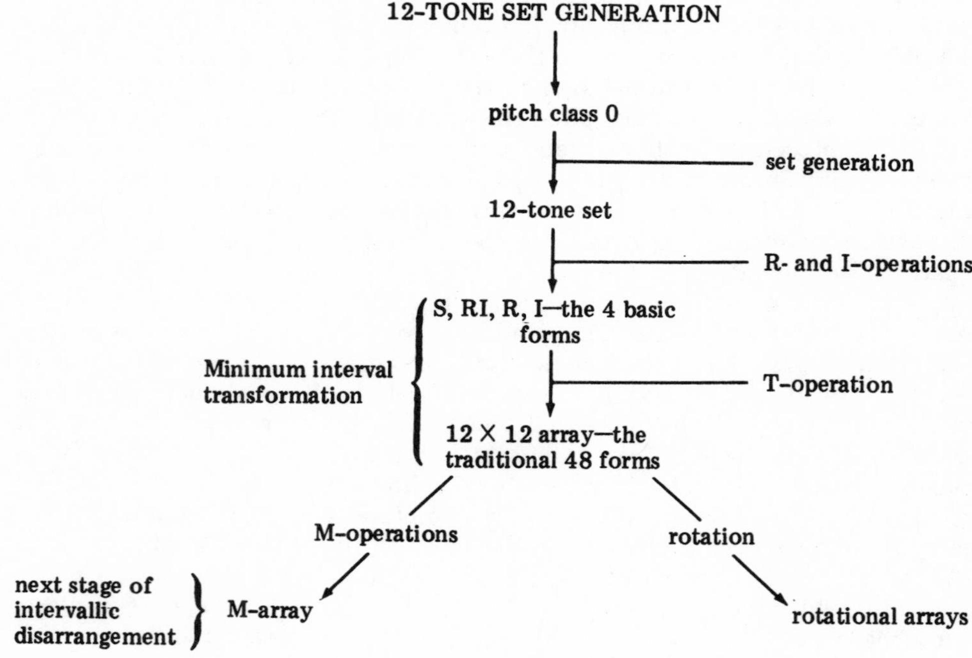

CHAPTER NINE

The 12-Tone Pitch System: Extensions

Now we come to an examination of certain general methods for extending the capacities and musical meaning of the 12-tone system. These methods depend on the operations described in chapters 6 and 7, and include *derivation* (the generation of new sets from segments, which may themselves be segments of other sets previously employed in a composition); *partitioning* (the slicing up of sets, successions of sets, or other arrays of pitch classes into constituent segments); and *combinatoriality* (certain properties of particular sets in their combination with other sets). We cannot attempt to treat these subjects exhaustively, as they are too broad, but the interested composer can find detailed information about them in the specialized professional literature. Here, we will only present a general outline and offer a few examples.

Derivation

The operations we have defined in chapters 6 and 7 can, as we know, apply to any pitch-class succession of any length; therefore, they may be used to transform *segments* of 12-tone sets as well as sets themselves. Example 75 displays a few such transformations of the trichord 0-4-3, with 0 here equal to G-natural:

EXAMPLE 75

EXERCISE Write out the following additional transformations of the trichord from example 75 (using note heads and pitch class numbers):
(a) T_{11} (b) RI_5 (c) R_6 (d) I_1 (e) $RM7_{11}$ (f) $M5_3$

The most important application of this method of transforming segments of less than twelve pitch classes consists in the selection of transformations such that several of them joined together will yield a new complete 12-tone set. (This new set is of course transformable itself by all the usual operations.) This device, first employed by Webern, is most commonly used with trichords, tetrachords, and hexachords, though it is of course possible to use other segments too. For instance, if we take the trichord in example 76-a and subject it successively to I_5, R_6, and RI_{11}, we obtain a total of four trichords—the original and three transformations—which when linked together yield a pitch content of all twelve pitch classes or, in other words, a new 12-tone set:

EXAMPLES 76a–b

The process of building up a new set out of segments which are 12-tone transformations of each other is *derivation;* and the newly generated set is called a *derived set.* Incidentally, note that the *order of segments* in the derived set is an open matter, and can be changed without affecting the total pitch content and, hence, the status of the new entity as a 12-tone set. Thus, we could have arranged the four trichords shown above as:

EXAMPLE 76–c

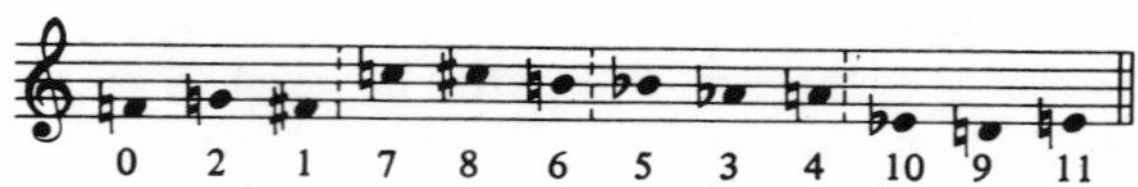

or as:

EXAMPLE 76–d

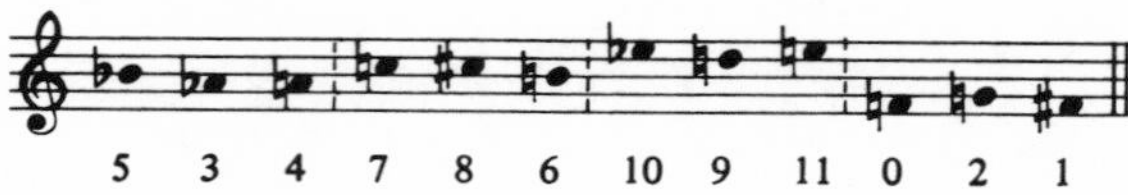

or twenty-two other rearrangements of the original ordering. (Since there are four trichords to be combined, there will be 4! or 24 possible orderings for their occurrence in the derived set.)

EXERCISE Write out in note heads and pitch class numbers the six arrangements of the four trichords above that have the generating trichord 0-2-1 at the beginning. (Two of these have already been given.)

Here is an illustration of a set generated from a tetrachord:

EXAMPLE 77

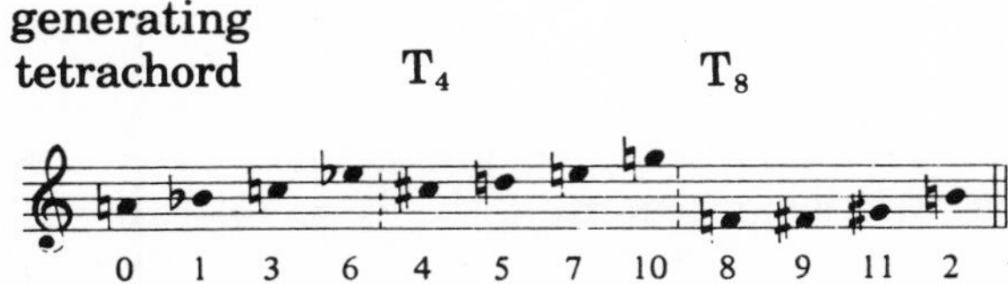

and one derived from a hexachord:

EXAMPLE 78

generating hexachord RI$_3$

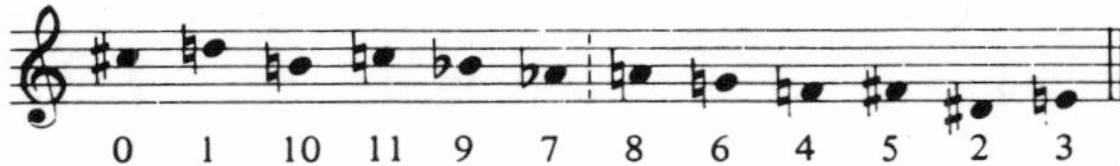

Hexachordally derived sets are less frequent than those generated from trichords and tetrachords; rarer still are sets derived from dyads or asymmetric divisions of 12-tone sets. Since trichordal and tetrachordal derivatives are the most important, certain special properties they exhibit should be pointed out:

1. A derived set can be generated by searching for appropriate combinations of T, R, and I from any trichord, with the single exception of the 0-3-6, or "diminished triad" trichord (example 79-a).
2. A derived set can be generated from any tetrachord that excludes the interval class 4 (a major third) from its constitutent intervals. It is essential to note that this means interval class 4 between *any* two elements in the tetrachord, not merely those that are adjacent to each other. Thus, for instance, 0-1-2-3 (example 79-b) contains no interval 4, and will generate a derived set; but 0-1-2-4 (example 79-c), although possessing no 4 between adjacent elements, nevertheless has a 4 between its first and its last, and therefore will not generate.

EXAMPLES 79a–c

What about compositional uses for these properties? One might, for example, have a set like the following as the basic set for a composition:

EXAMPLE 80

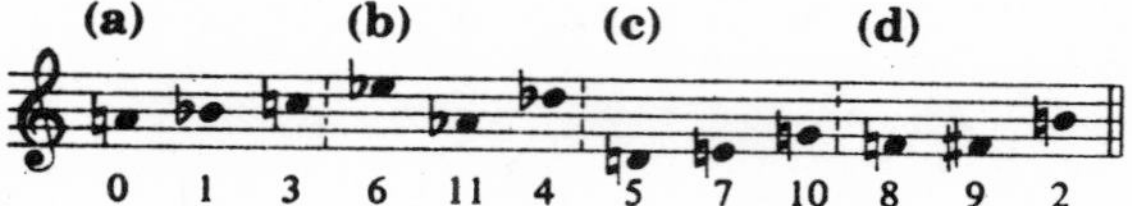

In this set, each trichord has a distinct interval content: There are 1's in the first trichord, 5's in the second, a 2 and a 3 in the third, and a 1 and a 5 in the fourth. (We are speaking here of uncomplemented interval classes.) Because of this characteristic—which is typical of the kind of thing one would build into the structure of the basic set for a piece, with an ear to capitalizing on it in the course of composing—one might want to expose the harmony that could be uniquely generated by each of the trichords, either in different sections of the composition or in juxtaposition and combination. For this, it would be reasonable to produce four derived sets, each generated by one of the trichords of the original, basic, set:

EXAMPLE 81 Sets derived from the four trichords of example 80.

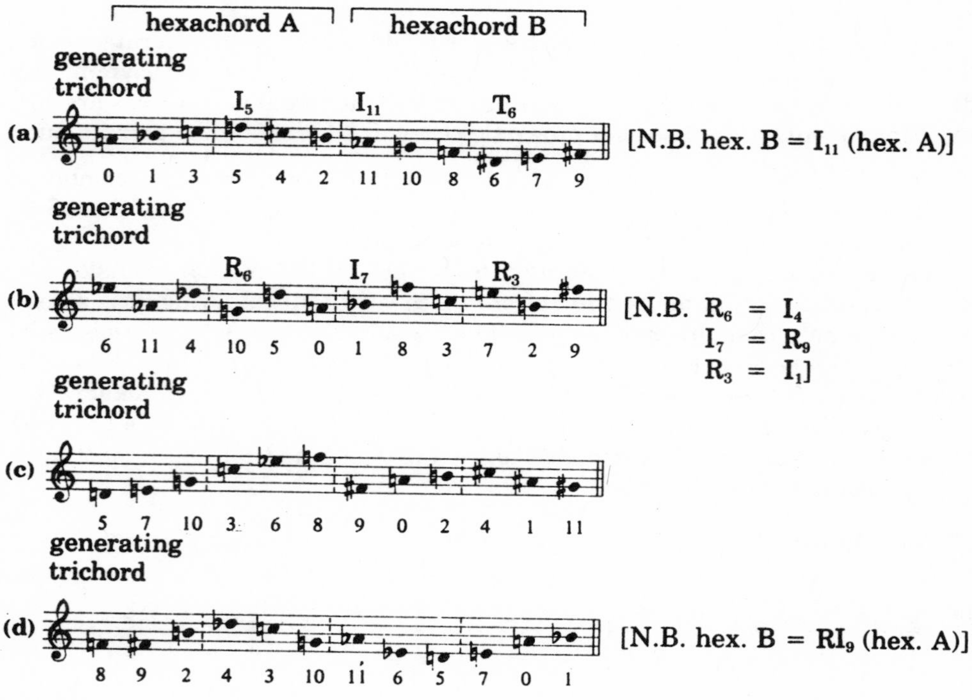

Each of the above derived sets could function locally in a particular region of the piece. Therefore, these derived sets would be hierarchically subsidiary to the main set for the whole work—distinct from it, yet related to it by common ancestry, with each derived set focusing on some special aspect of the original set. The process of derivation is yet another example of the way a simple construct—the original set—is ramified and multiplied into a much more complex entity by the application of a few simple processes. (Remember in this connection that each derived set can have its own arrays, rotations, etc.)

EXERCISES

1. From the following trichords and tetrachords, identify the ones that can be used to generate 12-tone sets. Where possible, perform the derivation. Make a 12 × 12 array for one each of the trichordally and tetrachordally derived sets. Now reorder the sequence of segments in the sets for which you made the arrays; make new arrays from these reorderings, and compare them with the original arrays.
   (a) Trichords:

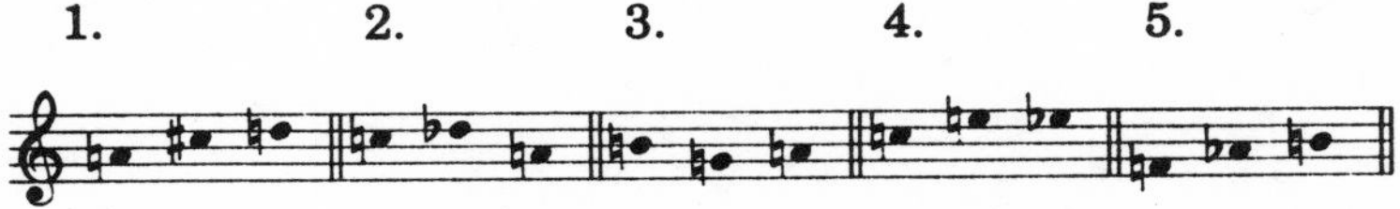

   (b) Tetrachords:

2. Make derived sets from the following hexachords:

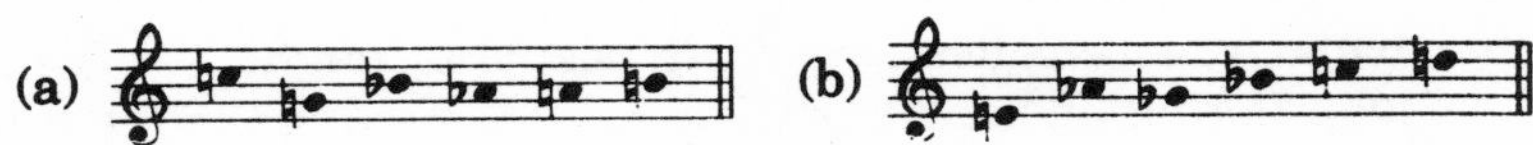

3. Make a 12 × 12 array for the set from exercise 2(a), above. How many *distinct* set-forms are there? What is the relation among duplicated forms?
4. Consider the set from example 80 and its derivatives in example 81. Write a short piece, specifying instrumentation (e.g., for piano) in six sections, the first and last using only the set from example 80 and the middle four using in succession the four derivatives in example 81. (The sections need not be set off from each other—i.e., the music may be continuous.)

Partitioning

In a sense, partitioning is the inverse of derivation, for while derivation builds up larger structures (12-tone sets) out of smaller, segmental generators, partitioning slices out subentities (such as segments) from larger ones (such as 12-tone sets). What is normally involved is the slicing-out of subsidiary lines from a larger single array of pitches. For example, the following diatonic line can be heard as the composite of two lines:

EXAMPLE 82–a

When one divides the single line above into two lines on the basis of registral separation, the following partition results:

EXAMPLE 82–b

Now there are many ways to execute partitioning, but by far the most common and successful is by means of *register*, just as we have done above. It is obvious why this should be so, for it is very easy to hear parts that are higher or lower than each other as separable components of the larger, more complex entity which together they constitute. What may be partitioned? Anything—but particularly, any collection of pitches. One might, for instance, take a single wide-ranging line and partition it (by assigning the different attacks in it to different voices) so that it comes to yield a multivoiced counterpoint. Thus, the following melodic line:

EXAMPLE 83–a

can be split up, or partitioned, into four voices:

EXAMPLE 83–b

The principle of partitioning in this example is simple: Each new attack of the original line goes to a different voice in the partition, barring only some minor exceptions involving repeated notes, and the following deviations: (measure 1) D-flat to C-natural in Flute IV to avoid the simultaneity of a minor second; (measure 2) E-natural to A-natural in Flute IV to preserve the slurring from the original single line, rather than have the E-natural sustained by another flute; (measure 3) B-flat to E-flat doubled in Flutes I and II for greater sonority; (measure 4) F-sharp doubled in Flutes II and III so that there can be a four-note chord to end on (the F-sharp could have been played by Flute II alone, but here my taste required a sostenuto line in Flute III to complement the motion of Flute IV).

For all this, however, we must remember that in this chapter we are not so much considering *notes* as we are, more abstractly, talking about pitch-class relationships. And therefore it is as an abstract and more general operation on pitch classes that we consider partitioning here. In particular, we will be interested in the process of segregating groups of pitch classes out of larger pitch-class successions or arrays.

It is possible to partition any 12-tone set into smaller segments. When we divide it up into its constituent dyads, trichords, tetrachords, or hexachords (as we have done in the preceding chapters), we are in fact partitioning it. But there are other more interesting ways to do this, which involve associating pitch classes from the set with others that are not necessarily adjacent. For example, if a 12-tone set is partitioned into dyads, all of one interval class, most or all of the six pairs formed by this method of association will consist of pitch classes not temporally adjacent to each other in that set. Example 84

nants of what is partitioned into what. Thus, the following line of music, which contains simultaneous attacks as some of its events:

EXAMPLE 86–a

is here sliced in such a way that one note is assigned to a given voice, the next note to a second voice, the next to a third voice, and so on in sequence among the three voices, thus changing it into three-part counterpoint:

EXAMPLE 86–b

EXERCISES

1. Partition each of the following sets into each of the uncomplemented interval classes (1/11, 2/10, 3/9, 5/7, 6—omitting 4/8 of course):

(a) 

(b) 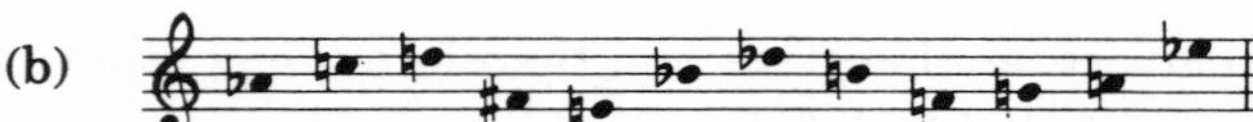

(c) 

2. Select one partition each from the three sets in exercise 1 above, and

write a short multivoiced phrase displaying the partitioning for each one.

3. Partition the following line into three voices, keeping the registral values as given:

4. Translate the following numerically notated pitch-class succession into note heads:

   0 11 7 8 10 9 1 6 2 4 5 3 / / 7 8 0 11 9 10 6 1 5 3 2 4 / /
   9 11 10 8 0 7 3 4 2 1 5 6 / / 10 8 9 11 7 0 4 3 5 6 2 1

   Now partition it, finding your own registral values to make good individual lines and overall harmony, into:

   (a) three-voiced counterpoint in which the notes are distributed in the order given, one at a time to each voice in turn (in the manner of examples 86-a and 86-b);

   (b) four-voice counterpoint in which the first two notes go to voice 1, the next note to voice 2, the next note to voice 3, the next two notes to voice 4, etc., repeating this pattern of note distribution until all the notes in the succession have been used.

   (The resulting lines need not be registrally separate, but when they overlap, they should behave according to the melodic principles sketched in chapter 5. Simultaneous attacks are possible.)

Questions How are the four set-forms that make up the material for exercise 4, above, related? In particular, what is the relation between the *second* hexachord of one form and the *first* of the one that follows it?

Combinatoriality

The atonal works of Schoenberg, which preceded his first efforts at formulating the 12-tone system, depend heavily on the contrapuntal combination of motives for their larger unfolding. It was natural, therefore, that when he began developing a compositional method based on 12-tone rows, his sense of what these pre-orderings were would still be fundamentally a motivic one—that is, although Schoenberg clearly saw the generality of interpretation possible for 12-tone sets, his own compositional use of them seemed to show that he was still most comfortable thinking of them as abstract motives, as pitch-class orderings that were most naturally expressible as *lines*. Indeed, even now, although we are more experienced with them and have a fuller understanding of how far-reaching the 12-tone system may be in its compositional influence, it is frequent to regard the set basically as a linear construct. It is in this spirit that we touch here on *combinatoriality,* which is the art of combining different set-forms or segments of them in such a way that the pitch-class content of the result fulfills certain criteria, which are determined in advance. Now while there are a great many elements and types of elements that can be combined (whole sets, segments of equal or unequal length, etc.) to result in a great many different possible collections of pitch classes, by far the most common concern lies in the combining of set segments (usually of equal length) whose total pitch-class content will add up exactly to the total chromatic.

Such a result—a collection of the twelve pitch classes without regard to their order of presentation—is called an *aggregate* (when the combination of contributing segments is simultaneous) or a *secondary set* (when the segments are joined to each other in succession). Example 87 illustrates this by combining a set S_0 with its untransposed retrograde R_0 and with itself:

EXAMPLE 87

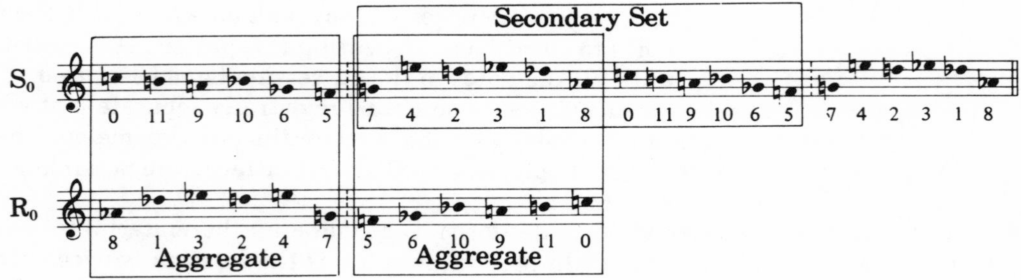

Notice the first six pitch classes (hexachords) of each set-form. Of course, the first six of the retrograde are the same (in content, not order) as the last six of S itself. Therefore, the first hexachords of each set, when taken together as shown, form the complete collection of twelve pitch classes—that is, an *aggregate.* Likewise for the second hexachord of each. Now examine the set followed by itself (i.e., all the pitch classes in the line marked S_0). If we take the second hexachord followed again by the first, we create a new ordering of the twelve pitch classes, consisting of some from one set and some from another (the fact that they are both S in this case is not important). This newly formed set is a *secondary set*. It is the result of combining segments of mutually exclusive pitch-class content, just as is an aggregate, but it differs from an aggregate in being an explicitly ordered entity taken as a whole; whereas segments combined to form aggregates are ordered only within themselves, not necessarily *between* each other (i.e., not as a whole).

The combinations illustrated in example 87 are actually trivial ones, demonstrating a property possessed by every 12-tone set, called *retrograde combinatoriality*. But there are certain sets which, because of the internal interval structure of their constituent segments, are capable of combining with many other transformations of themselves to form aggregates and secondary sets. Schoenberg, for example, made frequent use of sets which would form aggregates hexachordally with their own inversions transposed by a perfect fifth (i.e., with I_7), thus:

EXAMPLE 88

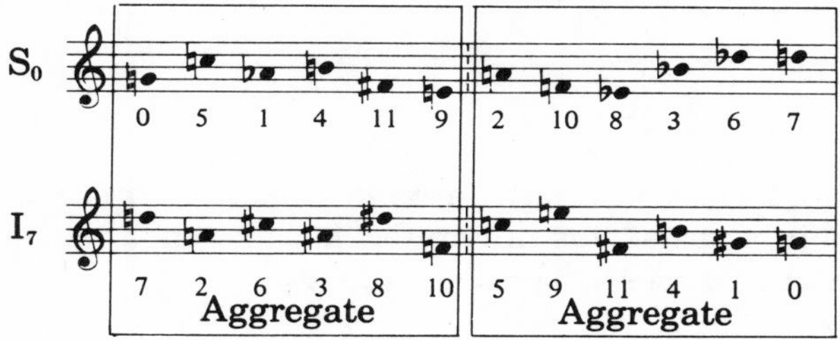

A set that is capable of combining with *one* of its four basic transformations, when that form is appropriately transposed, is called *semi-combinatorial*. One of these is shown in example 88. There is an even smaller number of sets that can be combined with *any* of the four basic mirror forms (S, RI, R, I) when these are given at appropriate transposition levels. These are called *all-combinatorial*. For instance, consider the following set:

EXAMPLE 89–a

This set will form hexachordal aggregates (such as those already illustrated) with itself at T_6; with its R at T_0; with its I at T_{11}; and with its RI at T_5. That is, S_0 forms aggregates with S_6, R_0, I_{11}, and RI_5. These are shown in example 89-b (except for R_0, because the aggregates produced by combining a set with its simple retrograde are trivial, as mentioned above):

EXAMPLE 89–b

In each case, two aggregates are formed, one each between respective first and second hexachords of the combining sets. One might also form secondary sets by following S_0 with these various forms retrograded—R_6, RI_{11}, or I_5.

EXERCISE Perform the retrogrades called for on the three forms that combine with S_0 in example 89-b. Write out S_0 three times, using three staves, in each case following it with one of the resulting forms. Mark off the secondary sets formed between the second hexachord of S_0 and the respective first hexachords of the following forms.

Even in the restricted way we have been considering combinatorial relations, it constitutes a vast subject. For one thing, there exist various types of sets that have more than one T-level available for each of the four basic forms in combinations. Moreover, combinatorial relations can be established for other types of sets divided into segments other than hexachords. Tetrachordal combinations, involving three set-forms each; trichordal combinations with four set-forms; dyads in combinations of six; and even monads (single pitch classes) in combinations of twelve—all of these exist and are often used.

Asymmetrical segmental divisions are also possible. Thus, for example, the following set is tetrachordally all-combinatorial:

EXAMPLE 90–a

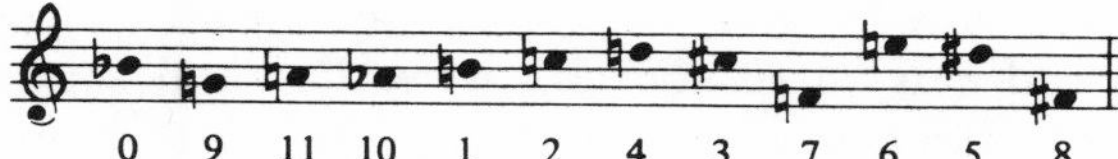

and will combine with two other of its transformations to form three tetrachordally generated aggregates, as follows:

EXAMPLE 90–b

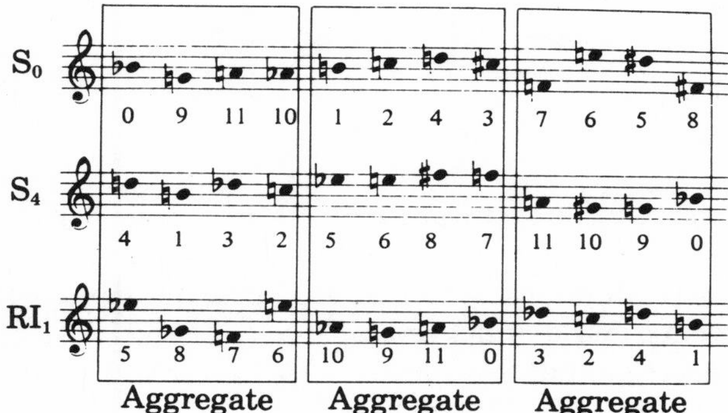

But clearly this subject is beyond our capacity to investigate in detail, and the interested composer is directed to more specialized and exhaustive treatments, some of which are listed in the Bibliography. It will be useful, however, to give a summary table of the six basic hexachordally all-combinatorial sets, called *source sets* in this presentation. They were first identified and tabulated in this form by Milton Babbitt:

EXAMPLE 91

(A) 0 1 2 3 4 5 // 6 7 8 9 10 11
(B) 0 2 3 4 5 7 // 6 8 9 10 11 1
(C) 0 2 4 5 7 9 // 6 8 10 11 1 3
(D) 0 1 2 6 7 8 // 3 4 5 9 10 11
(E) 0 1 4 5 8 9 // 2 3 6 7 10 11
(F) 0 2 4 6 8 10 // 1 3 5 7 9 11

There are several things to notice about this tabulation. First, we give the sets numerically only, for that way they can be stated at any transpositional level we choose. Next, and most important: It is the interval *content* (that is, the total of intervals between every possible pair of elements, not just adjacent ones; with hexachords, there are fifteen such possible intervals), not interval order, that determines combinatorial properties. Therefore, in the table, the two hexachords of each set are given only in their "simplest," scalar ordering. The pitch classes of each hexachord can be reordered *internally* (and separately) in any way we wish without changing any of their combinatorial properties. (Since there are six elements in a hexachord, there exist 6! or 720 possible orderings.) Therefore, each of the sets in our list really stands for 720 orderings × 2 hexachords × 12 possible transpositional levels on which to start, the product of which is 17,280 possible distinct sets. There are 6 × 17,280—or 103,680—hexachordally all-combinatorial sets, if we consider all of the six source sets in the table together. The designation "source set" is used because each of the listed sets actually represents so many possible distinct orderings.

EXERCISES

1. Transcribe the source sets listed in example 91 into note heads, once with 0 = C-natural and once with 0 = F-sharp.
2. Write out two different orderings for each of your transcriptions, yielding a total of twenty-four distinct sets.
3. In its "simplest" ordering, what is source set (A)? Source set (C)? Source set (F)?

Continuing our consideration of example 91, we should point out that the source sets are ranked according to the number of possible T-levels they possess for hexachordal combinatoriality—one, two, three, or six. And notice that as we progress from set (A), which forms aggregates at only one T-level for each of its transformations to set (F), which forms them at six T-levels, the increase in available transpositions is complemented by a decrease in intervallic variety within the hexachords—that is, a decrease in the number of different distinct intervals. Thus, in set (A), the chromatic hexachords that constitute it can be ordered so that they contain every interval class except the tritone:

EXAMPLE 92–a

intervals (uncomplemented)

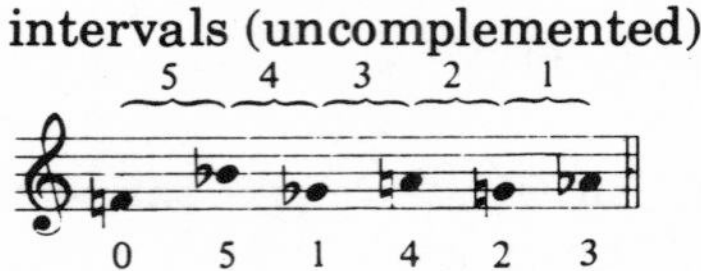

but the last set (F), consisting of two whole-tone hexachords, excludes within each hexachord all interval classes containing minor seconds—that is, contains only even interval classes:

EXAMPLE 92–b

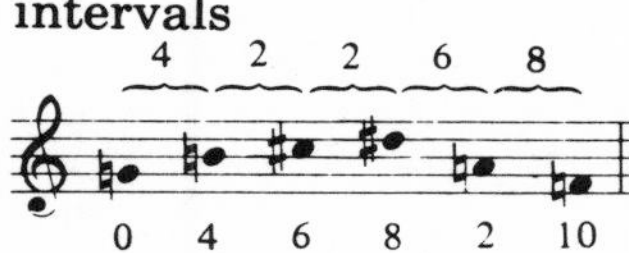

EXERCISE Following the patterns started in the hexachords given in examples 92-a and 92-b, complete their respective second hexachords.

Remarks

How are these relationships useful in composing music? Clearly the answer must lie in the desirability of controlling the pitch-class content of a succession or progression so that the harmony may unfold as the composer desires. By far the most common practice is to arrange combinatorial relations so that they bring about a progression in *aggregates,* when two or more set-forms are combined simultaneously; or in *secondary sets,* when two combinatorially related set-forms succeed each other. Thus is created a progression in units each of which makes up the total chromatic. This is regarded as desirable, and has often been justified on the grounds that it represents an analogy with harmonic progression in the tonal system. I have doubts about the validity of such a comparison, however: Harmonic progression in tonal music means above all moving from one domain (say, that of a tonic triad) to another (say, that of a dominant), which differs from the first in precisely defined ways (here, by incomplete intersection of pitch-class content and exactly defined transpositional and intervallic relations). Progression in aggregates or through secondary sets means only that bundles of pitch classes, each consisting of the total available pitch class vocabulary, will succeed each other. The usefulness of aggregate and secondary set progression seems somewhat dubious on perceptual grounds as well, for, since it is normally quite difficult to tell in a texture of any contrapuntal complexity whether there really are twelve (as opposed to eleven, ten, or even nine) distinct pitch classes present, the question may be raised whether these kinds of successions are perceptually very useful. But in voicing these reserves, I hasten to remind the reader that the methods involved may still be of great *compositional* importance. Just because perception is not directly involved here does not mean that a composer who employs these relations will not be constructively disciplined by using them. For *him*, they may be of enormous structural and methodological significance. And this is his right, since he is the one writing the piece.

Here is a simple example of how a number of set-forms, here treated as models or sketches of contrapuntal lines, can be combined to yield a progression in aggregates and secondary sets:

EXAMPLE 93

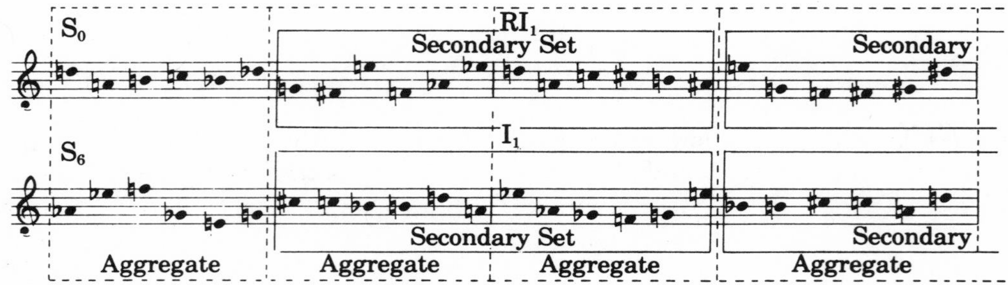

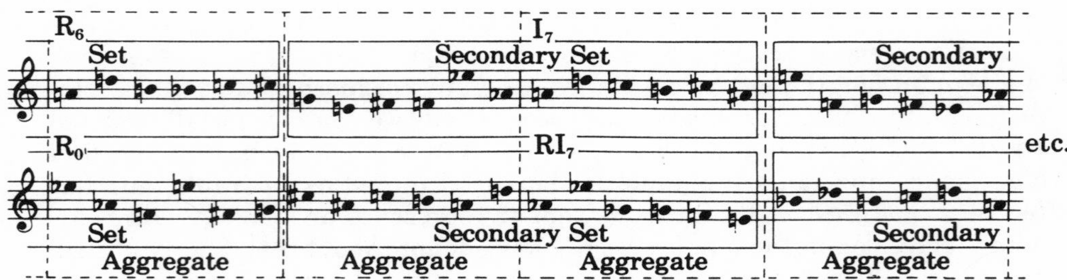

In this example we have restricted ourselves to two voices, which most naturally involves hexachordal combinatoriality.

EXERCISES

1. Translate the pitch classes of example 93 into pitch class numbers, mapped out in an arrangement showing the two voices.
2. Transcribe the map you made in exercise 1, above, into notes again, this time with 0 = C-natural. Give rhythmic, registral, and articulative values, thus transforming the pitch-class succession into actual two-voice counterpoint. Make your setting for two similar instruments (e.g., two flutes, two trombones, etc.).

3. Refer to example 91. Make an ordering (not one you have made before) for each of the six source sets. Then, form hexachordal aggregates with a transposition of each of every set's four basic forms (i.e., combine your orderings of each source set with S, RI, R, and I, successively.)

CHAPTER TEN

Rhythmic Organization: The Time-Point System

So far, our consideration of 12-tone organization has dealt only in a general way with questions of rhythm. While it is perfectly possible to continue to make rhythmic choices by contextual and intuitive means (since the role of rhythm is really in support of pitch relations), we should nevertheless have available a somewhat more precisely organized way of deciding rhythmic gestures—one that is correlated with the pitch relations of the 12-tone system and more directly generated by its relationships—than the means we have employed up to now. For this purpose, we introduce here the *time-point system*, which was first developed by Milton Babbitt.

Before describing this system, we should stress that it is both flexible and expansible, like the 12-tone pitch system from which it is derived. When we speak about it, we no more wish to imply a rigidly constrained or limited method of organization than we have in talking about the 12-tone pitch system.

Fundamental Principles

The time-point system rests upon two fundamental principles:

1. The relationships of the pitch system are transferred in their totality to the sphere of time relations.
2. This transfer is accomplished through the linkage of one simple equivalence—that of *time interval* corresponding to *pitch interval*.

As we discuss these transfers from the domain of pitch to that of time, the great advantage, indeed indispensability, of numerical notation will become quickly evident.

How is musical time different from pitch? Aside from the fact that it is (in musical terms) a manifestation of pitch and therefore not co-equal with it, we can make other constructive distinctions—for example, we can think of time as the "horizontal" dimension of music, and pitch as the "vertical." The following diagram shows this:

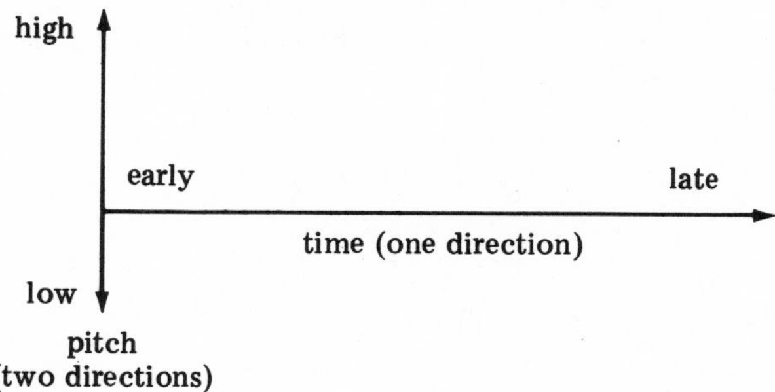

If we represent time/pitch relations as above, we ought to note something else critical for musical purposes: Time is one-directional, pitch is not. Pitch successions can have two directions, upward or downward; but time goes forward only. But time and pitch have one critical element in common: They are both continuums which are divided up for musical purposes by *intervals*. A pitch interval is the distance between two pitches (or more abstractly, the interval class separating two pitch classes). A time interval is the distance (or time length) between two *time points*. What is a time point? Simply a *location* in the flow of time. In music, such a location is only recognizable if it is defined by an *event*. Such an event may be the beginning of something (like an attack), the end of something (like a release), the point at which something changes (such as a change in dynamic level during a sustained note). But by far the most common event that defines the location of a time point in music will be the first one just mentioned—the *attack-point* of a note.

Let us turn back now to the 12-tone pitch system. If we want to, we can consider it as made up of intervals, and its constitutent pitch classes or pitches as *points* defining these intervals. When we do so, it becomes easy to transfer all the relations and operations which we have already described in the pitch system directly into the domain of time. To accomplish this, we establish the following correlations between the two areas:

TIME	←——→	PITCH
Time point (specific location in time)	←——→	Pitch (a specific note)
Time point class (to be defined)	←——→	Pitch class
Durational interval	←——→	Interval (between two specific notes)
Durational interval class	←——→	Interval class

Notice that we are effecting our transfer by correlating locations in one area (pitches) with locations in the other (time points). Most emphatically, notice that with regard to the events whose initiations mark off the time intervals, *duration,* i.e., note length—as opposed to durational interval—*has no basic role.* The following example illustrates the point by showing that, despite the great variety in the durations of the two pitches that define the time interval, it is nevertheless always the same, because the distance between their attacks is always the same:

EXAMPLE 94

Now in effecting our transfer of relations and operations from the sphere of pitch to that of time, another crucial difference between the two must strike us: Whether by convention or by divine ordinance, the pitch continuum is modularly divided, into octaves, each of which contains the same internal 12-part equal-interval division. As we have seen, it is this sense of modular division that enables us to think of groupings of octave-related pitches as being equivalent in function—this is the principle of octave equivalence. But in the flow of musical time, there is no such *a priori* modular division. Musical time is not divided up in advance for us into any particular units. Such division, whether of beats and meters in the traditional, periodic sense, or more aperiodically in the manner we have discussed earlier, must be imposed on the undivided time continuum afresh for each piece. As we attempt to transfer characteristics of the pitch system into time-organizing terms, we therefore will have to impose an "artificial" modular division scheme on the flow of musical time. But since this imposition is special to every particular work, rather than general and independent (the way the pitch octave is), questions about its size, the number of its internal intervallic divisions, and even whether it should be constant in magnitude, are all open, contextual, and subject to local considerations.

To effect our relational transfer, then, we have to assert a modulus for the flow of time, to correspond to the pitch octave. The most obvious way to do this (and the one followed by Babbitt in his development of the system) is to select a modulus (therefore of constant size), divided internally into twelve equal parts. Then the time continuum will be divided intervallically *mod* 12 just as is the pitch continuum, and the twelve internal divisions of the time modulus will therefore make up twelve time-point classes, which can be correlated 1:1 with the twelve pitch classes. But always bear in mind that while the *mod* 12 pitch system is external, in Western music, to the specific piece, the temporal modulus is a "personal" choice—and its justification is logic and convenience, not convention and tradition. Even within this framework, moreover, time points could be nicely represented *mod* 6, *mod* 4, or *mod* 3, and still make all the relational transfers we have been anticipating take place without difficulty. Indeed, the time-point system is often used this way.

In example 95, we show diagrammatically the correspondences we have been discussing. Here, two things are arbitrary: (1) the choice of F-natural as the boundary for the pitch octave, and (2) the choice of a 𝅗𝅥. (or 12 ♪'s) as the temporal modulus. Tempo has not been specified either:

EXAMPLE 95

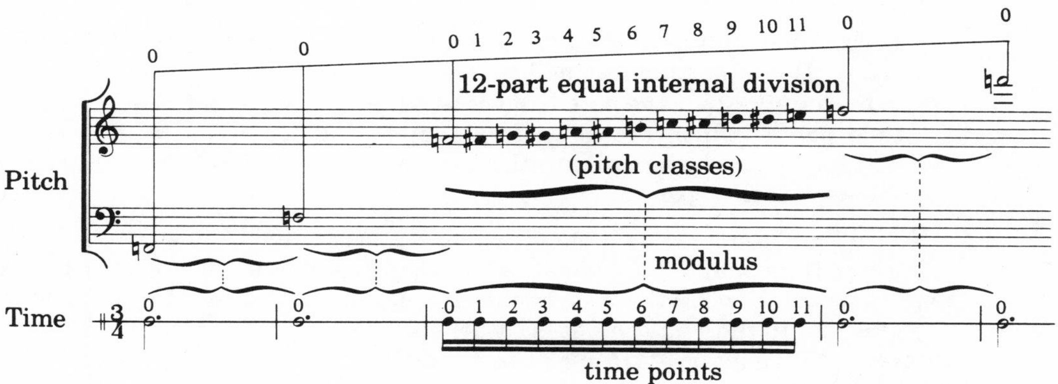

Let us begin our transfer of pitch to time by translating the following pitch-class succession (in this case a 12-tone set) into a time-point succession, also *mod* 12, using the same time modulus used in example 95. Thus:

EXAMPLE 96–a

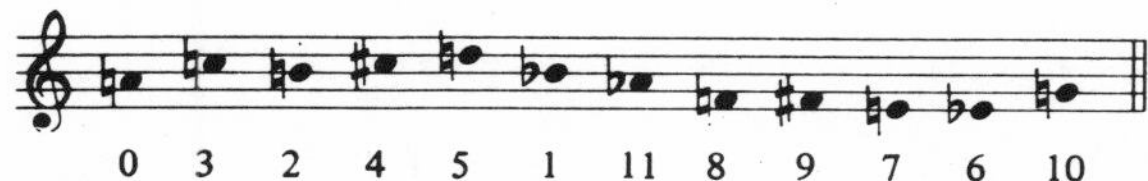

can be translated numerically as:

EXAMPLE 96–b

	0	3	(2 + 12)	(4 + 12)	(5 + 12)	(1 + 24)	(11 + 24)	etc.
or:	0	3	14	16	17	25	35	etc.
or, *mod* 12:	0	3	2	4	5	1	11	etc.

and notated rhythmically as:

EXAMPLE 96–c

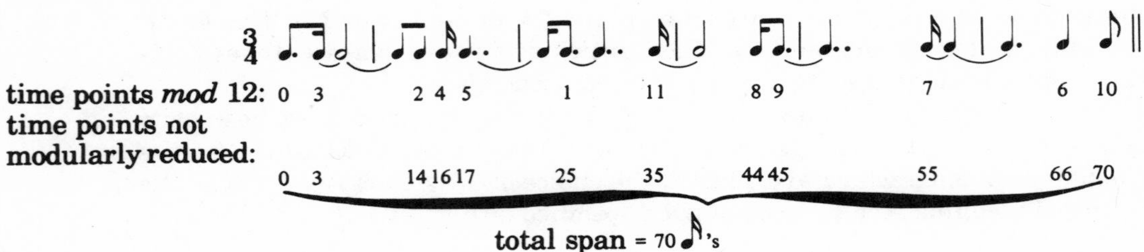

In this manner we have created a *time-point set* that corresponds to our original pitch set. (Note that:

> **1.** Example 96-b is an arithmetic way, *mod* 12, of showing that the time intervals are continuously additive.
> **2.** In example 96-c, the note lengths serve *only* to show the locations of the time points, which are at each of the attacks. The note lengths imply nothing about the actual durations of the events that may be initiated at the several time points.)

Notice that because time is one-directional, there is only one way to position any given time point—i.e., *after* the one that precedes it. This means that a time point number less than the one it precedes must be embedded in the next modulus, not in the same one. It is rather as if one had to express a succession of tones with the intervals in one direction only—so that the option of placing a tone (i.e., expressing an interval class) above or below its predecessor was not available, and one could only place it, say, above. Consider the time-point succession 0-3-2, shown as:

EXAMPLE 97–a

3/4 etc.

0 3 2

Unless time point 2 is placed in the modular measure immediately after that containing time point 3, an erroneous representation would result, as:

EXAMPLE 97–b

3/4 etc.

0 2 3

which disarranges the time-point succession as 0-2-3.

EXERCISES

1. Translate the following pitch-class succession into time points. Proceed by first re-expressing the pitch classes numerically.

Then, interpret the numbers as time points and write them out as in example 96-c. Do this (assuming a tempo of ♩=60) with the following moduli:
   (a) $\frac{3}{4}$ divided into twelve 𝅘𝅥𝅯 's
   (b) $\frac{4}{4}$ divided into twelve ³♪ 's
   (c) $\frac{6}{4}$ divided into twelve ♪ 's

2. Now, reduce the succession of time point numbers from exercise 1 above, using *mod* 6. There will only be values 0 through 5, and there will be two of each. (For example, 0 9 2 4 5 11 1 8 3 7 6 10 *mod* 6 is 0 3 2 4 5 5 1 2 3 1 0 4. The same succession *mod* 3 is 0 0 2 1 2 2 1 2 0 1 0 1.)
3. Write out the time points again, now *mod* 6, in moduli of:
   (a) $\frac{3}{4}$ divided into twelve sixteenth-notes
   (b) $\frac{3}{8}$ divided into twelve thirty-second-note
4. Repeat exercise 3 above, only now use *mod* 3.
5. Return to the original *mod* 12 succession and write it out with moduli of alternating size: $\frac{3}{4}$ $\frac{4}{4}$ $\frac{3}{4}$ $\frac{4}{4}$ etc. Each measure, though of different size, will always be divided into twelve equal intervals—$\frac{4}{4}$ into twelve ³♪ 's, $\frac{3}{4}$ into twelve 𝅘𝅥𝅯 's, etc.

(Note that although the locations of the time points are quantitatively determined, it is the order of their succession, more than the durational intervals among them, that give coherence. For this reason, the deforming effect of variable temporal moduli is not serious.)

6. Refer to example 93. Express the two voices in that example as time-point set successions. Attach its corresponding pitch class to each time point. Give registral values, articulation, tempo, etc.

Elements and Operations

We are now in a position to describe the relation between the elements and operations of the pitch system and those of the time system. The principle is simple: Since we have already defined all of the elements and operations of the pitch system in numerical terms, we don't have to bother redefining them for a temporal context—and many of them have no intuitively obvious temporal analogy anyway. All we have to do is to express the *results* of the operations as time-point successions rather than as pitch-class successions. Thus, for every operation and every set-form in one domain, there is an exact equivalent in the other. The operations T, R, I, RI, M7, etc., as well as their combinations, all have precise meanings and expressions in the temporal sphere; but note most importantly that these are not always the ones that seem at first the most obvious. Thus, for example, the retrograde of a time-point succession is *not* the retrograde of the "durations" between successive time points, it is the retrograde of the time points *themselves*. And just as the interval succession of a retrograded pitch-class series is the RI of the interval succession of the unretrograded series, so are the time intervals between successive time points under R changed as well (to their complements). Observe, then, that when:

EXAMPLE 98–a

is expressed as a time-point set:

EXAMPLE 98–b

the retrograde of this latter is:

EXAMPLE 98–c

(Notice that the interval succession is the reverse-complement of that for S_0. For instance, the first interval of S_0 is 0-10, which is a 10. The last interval in R_0, which corresponds to it, is, however, 10-0, which is a 2, the complement of 10.)

EXERCISE Make a table of interval sizes, comparing corresponding intervals in examples 98-b and 98-c (first of S_0 with last of R_0, etc.). What is the relation between the elements in these pairs of intervals?

We see, then, that temporal retrogression is not a simple reversal of durations, as it might at first appear to be. Now if we go on to inversion, we have an even more difficult situation, for there is no intuitively obvious meaning for I in temporal terms. But if we remember I defined as complementation of pitch class numbers *mod* 12, we need only substitute "time point" for "pitch class," and the temporal meaning for I—that is, complementation—is established. Thus, example 99 is I_0 of example 98-b:

EXAMPLE 99

Let us note once more the tremendous power given us by a neutral representation and a generalized definition of fundamental operations and elements. Here, because of numerical notation and definition, we can effortlessly transfer the entire apparatus of relationships from pitch to time. And indeed it should be noted that *any* such transfer out of the pitch domain to some other is equally possible, provided only that: (1) the principle of correlation is a sound one; and (2) the transfer seems potentially fruitful for composing.

In the following examples, we summarize the entire array of operations we have previously described for pitch-class sets (except for rotation, which is left as something the reader can do on his own), now given as temporal equivalents. Here, as in the immediately preceding examples, each time point is correlated with its corresponding pitch class. For brevity, we will use a hexachord instead of a 12-tone set:

EXAMPLE 100–a

The interval-class succession of this hexachord is 10-11-2-3-3. Example 100-b shows I_0 of example 100-a. Look at the durational intervals, and you will see that they are the complements of those of the original hexachord—namely, 2-1-10-9-9:

EXAMPLE 100–b

Example 100-c shows R_0:

EXAMPLE 100–c

and observe that the intervals are reversed *and* complemented: 9-9-10-1-2. The RI_0 transformation given as:

EXAMPLE 100–d

also shows something about the closeness of S and RI: Under RI, the interval succession of S is merely reversed: 3-3-2-11-10. Example 100-e shows transposition, here T_4. In temporal terms, T merely reorients the time-point succession by shifting everything a certain interval later within the flow of modular measures; in example 100-e, the original succession of time points is shifted four sixteenths later. The intervals themselves remain unaltered:

EXAMPLE 100–e

Finally, we give a transformation under M7. Here the intervals are 10-5-2-9-9, the M7 of those of the original hexachord:

EXAMPLE 100–f

Time-Pitch Correlation

In order to complete our discussion of the transfer of relations and operations from the domain of pitch to the domain of time, we must present the correlation of actual pitch classes or notes with time points. There is an infinity of ways to do this. A time-point set may be correlated 1:1 with its pitch class equivalent:

EXAMPLE 101-a

A time-point set may be correlated with pitch classes from another set-form:

EXAMPLE 101-b

In example 101-b, the time points are correlated with pitch classes of the corresponding retrograde form.

More, or less, than one new pitch class may be attached to each time point. In example 101-c, the time points are those of example 101-b, and so are the pitch classes, but the latter are now redistributed so that some time points have more than one pitch class attached to them, and others repeat a pitch class already stated:

EXAMPLE 101–c

Time points can represent something other than the attacks of notes:

EXAMPLE 101–d

Example 101-d takes the time-point succession of example 101-b and uses it to define: (1) dynamic changes, and (2) instrumental entrances—all on a single note.

A combination of time-point set-forms may have pitch classes from the same combination of set-forms attached to it, but not in a 1:1 fashion. In example 102, the two voices have their rhythm from S_0 and I_0 simultaneously unfolded. The pitches also come from S_0 and I_1 (in reverse order so that I_1 comes first), but successively unfolded instead, each new attack in either voice receiving the next pitch class. As a final complication, we embed all this in a variable temporal modulus (measure 1 = 12 ♪'s, measure 2 = 12 ³♪'s, measure 3 = 12 𝅘𝅥𝅯's, etc.):

EXAMPLE 102

EXERCISES

1. Translate example 102 into pitch class numbers, each paired with the time point number associated with its attack. Compare the succession of time point numbers with that of the pitch class numbers.
2. Make an articulated piece for two instruments out of the pitch-class/time-point succession represented in example 102. Make sure that the durations of tones do not slavishly follow the durational intervals between attacks.

The illustrations above show that time-point sets are essentially independent of pitch-class sets, and that the correlation between them is variable, subject to infinite nuance, and dependent not upon formula, but upon reason and good compositional judgment. To encourage the latter, we append the following further exercises:

EXERCISES

1. Make a 12×12 array from the following set:
   0 4 2 7 9 5 6 10 11 1 3 8
2. Write out in time-point/pitch-class form, with a modulus of constant size, the following:
   S_0 R_6 S_6 I_3
3. Write out the following combination forms:

	Pitch classes		*Time points*
(a)	S_0	correlated with	I_3
(b)	R_6	correlated with	S_6
(c)	S_6	correlated with	R_6
(d)	I_3	correlated with	S_0

4. Combine the results of exercise 3, above, contrapuntally, as follows:
   Voice I : (a)—(b)
   Voice II: (c)—(d)
5. Articulate the results of exercise 4, above, into real music, for two celli.

PART IV
Form

CHAPTER ELEVEN *Form and Composition*

We are about to consider ways of making whole pieces, ways to organize the various matters of detail we have already discussed into coherent and pleasingly unfolding wholes. It seems permanently paradoxical that although the large form of musical compositions is their most difficult aspect, and success with them the truest test of compositional distinction, we must begin the study of composition not with this fundamental matter, but with specific, concrete musical situations that can be grasped directly and intuitively by one who has not yet developed a capacity for large-scale compositional abstraction. But we must come to terms with these larger matters, and in the following pages I shall present a few methods (out of a potentially infinite number) to make large pieces. First, to the consideration of some general points:

The perception of large musical form of course results from the accretion of a multitude of detailed relations among the concrete entities that make up a work—the various tones and their locations in time, along with their other sonic characteristics. But we also think musically in large gestural shapes or unfoldings, and the exploitation of these, as well as the definition of new ones, has produced much excellent music. In Western music as a whole (and in much non-Western music, too), the overall shape of a work seems to be perceived largely in terms of its development toward a focal or high point, or climax, whether the work is a single line that rises to a high point shortly before its end, or a large symphonic piece with its climactic intensification at the close. How such a sense of culmination is achieved cannot be divorced from the musical system employed in the work where it is located. But in general, we might characterize the sense of large formal process implicit in the work as "developmental," for the musical material is usually "developed" in the following manner: presented in an exposition, then transformed in some way which, contextually, seems to intensify it, and brought to a close, the arrival of which is in turn "justified" by the acts of intensification which had preceded it. One example of this lies in the "development sections" of certain tonal sonata movements, where harmonic instability (as defined by the relations of tonality) is succeeded by the tonally unambiguous return of the exposition material. Another may be found in Bach's fugal stretti.

How far do these formal patterns persist in music today? I believe that they still underlie almost all compositional activity, but that often they are much more subtly expressed than they were in the past. Furthermore, there is at least one major twentieth-century contribution to the storehouse of large formal patterns, and it often seems to complement the developmental continuity we have been considering. Indeed, the influence of this second type probably interpenetrates with the first in most pieces composed nowadays. This second type is a continuity made by the juxtaposition of dissimilar elements. Archetypal examples of these two major kinds of continuity from our era may be found in Stravinsky for the juxtapositional, and Schoenberg for the developmental. Schoenberg follows developmental gestural-shape processes taken over from the Germanic tradition with often surprisingly little alteration in their essential characteristics. But Stravinsky, as is well known, frequently resorts to sharp cleavages of musical continuity—abrupt ruptures of the pitch-relational fabric and of the instrumental, textural, articulative flow. And frequently in his music, the large form results from the juxtaposition of dissimilar entities whose constant recombination and simultaneous individual transformation completes the sense of form for the work—the sense of having moved from somewhere to somewhere else, and (sometimes) back again as well to the original state.

These two types of continuity are available to us in our formal adventures; and the use of one need not prevent the use of the other. Thus, for instance, if we make the large form of a work dependent on the expanded time-point system described in Chapter 12, we will presumably have a "developmental" continuity. But since the articulation, registration, instrumentation, phrasing, etc., of such a schema would not yet have been selected, we might well choose to slice it articulatively so that the immediate foreground might feature apparent sharp breaks in continuity—"dramatic" breaks. In this way the two approaches would be combined, with the underlying substructure given by the time-point/pitch-class unfolding that was plotted out in advance. As an example, consider:

EXAMPLE 103–a

which is a simple (to say the least) pitch-class succession, articulated in a seemingly "continuous" fashion. But it could be registrally articulated to be sharply disjunct:

EXAMPLE 103–b

Even though the registral changes from example 103-a to example 103-b set up subsidiary pitch and time relations not present in the original, the basic time-point/pitch-class scheme remains in force, so that despite the seeming articulative (registral) discontinuity of example 103-b, it remains a coherent whole. The notion illustrated here can easily be transferred to the scale of whole compositions. (Certain techniques for doing this are given in chapter 12.)

Here I want to offer some general advice. Naturally, these recommendations have less than universal applicability, but they may be helpful in a number of cases of compositional perplexity.

One of the most common difficulties young composers face arises from the mistaken assumption that composition is the same as slowed-down listening: that the work being composed should unfold in the mind's ear just as it would if it were being performed, then to be written down (by dictation, as it were, from the Muse). Now while one may often have flashes of insight that make possible the begetting and quick writing down of ideas in a nearly complete form, one cannot always count on such metaphysical assistance in the day-to-day work of writing music. Most of the time (unless one is living, as we are not, in an age governed by universally accepted detailed musical conventions) one must figure things out more slowly. It is in this condition that the myth of composition as slowed-down listening becomes pernicious. For it leads composers to try to through-compose—i.e., write pieces in the order in which they will be played, from beginning to end, and write them from the outset at a degree of completeness far beyond their grasp of what the piece will ultimately require in matters of detail.

It is therefore perhaps better to follow the suggestions given below, always remembering, however, that they are general but not universal:

1. Compose from the large into the small. That is, fix in a general way the general relations of the piece first. (Naturally, this may involve choosing specific motivic materials, 12-tone sets, and other fundamental constructs on which the piece is to be based; the fact that some of these may be represented as small-scale concrete musical entities does not diminish their generality.)

2. Try to keep all regions of the piece always in the same degree of completeness. As a rule, avoid defining one part precisely while at the same time leaving another blank. At the beginning of composing, let the whole work be vaguely defined in general terms. Let each subsequent operation apply over the whole work, or a major subdivision of it. Thus all regions of the piece gradually achieve concreteness at the same time.

3. To implement this second suggestion, above, make use of multiple successive drafts of the composition. Make an initial draft or diagram or outline governing the whole work. Then proceed to a preliminary sketch, which embodies only rough outlines. Do not fear repeated drafts, each of which is only a little more exact, precise, and complete than its predecessor. Often, writing things out again is the best way of clarifying problems, and renotating often brings insight in surprising ways.

4. By means of the foregoing three suggestions, view the piece whole and entire. At each stage of the compositional process, try to have the same degree of knowledge and awareness of all the regions of the work, the end as clearly (or as vaguely) as the beginning. This will give you a sense of the work independent of time; for you as its maker, it can all be encompassed instantaneously—you do not have to "listen" to it in your mind's ear to know what it contains. As we observed at the beginning of this book, it is this instantaneous perception of all parts of the work at once, independent of time, which distinguishes composing from all other musical acts. The capacity to apprehend musical relations in this way is not encouraged in most musical education and discourse. Alas! For it is vital to compositional success, and each one who would compose must find it in his own way and labor, alone, to sharpen its power.

5. A compositional method exists only to write pieces. It is not sacred, and when the piece has reached, through application of the method, a sufficient degree of completeness, it will begin to assert its own rights and needs. These may often seem to contradict the original method or call for changes in the work's design. Do not hesitate when such a situation arises. If the method has served long enough to allow the work it has produced to contradict it, it has more than fulfilled its function.

CHAPTER TWELVE

Formal Organization: Extending the Time-Point System

The discussion of the time-point system in chapter 10 carried with it the implication that time-point sets (and for that matter, pitch-class sets, too) are essentially local or small-scale entities, mainly useful for producing a coherent note-to-note continuity within the larger design of a composition. Indeed, this has been their main use in the past, though not their exclusive one. But as we mentioned in chapter 10, they can also function on a larger scale, where their interval successions, whether of time or pitch, may span larger sections of a piece than the immediate foreground of an immediate neighborhood—or perhaps even span the whole piece itself.

The fact remains, however, that everything we have done so far has been based on proceeding from small-scale to large—that is, our sets and other successions are regarded (however abstractly) as local entities, many of which have to be combined successively and simultaneously to yield a larger whole. Now while the time-point system as outlined above, complete with its time-modular intervals, may be expanded to a scale that might govern large-scale unfolding and subsume many smaller events (such as complete set-forms) in the generosity of its spread, the means for extending it in this way can become very complicated. If we wish to consider the time-point/pitch-class correlation from a large-scale point of view, as well as to prepare ourselves for its actual use in generating *form*, it will be convenient to try another approach which is essentially the complement of what we have just been describing.

Basic Divisions: From Sectional Structure to Foreground Rhythm

We have observed that the Babbittonian formulation of the time-point system implies a progress of mosaic-like accretion—small units of continuity (pitch-class/time-point set-form complexes) are conjoined to make a larger continuity. The large is built up out of, and gradually emerges from, the manipulation of small entities. In the alternative method I am about to outline, one takes the reverse approach, beginning with large spans (usually the entire extent of the work to be composed or perhaps a major subdivision of it, such as a movement), which are only defined in the most general way (usually only with regard to length), and proceeding through a process of refinement to slice out progressively more exact and concrete detail until the small-scale aspects of the work emerge from the larger generalities.

Here, just as in our previous use of the time-point system, intervals of pitch have as their temporal correlates durational intervals (intervals of time), but with two essential differences:

1. The scale on which the intervallic division begins is vastly greater than before, amounting now to the extent of the whole work, rather than to that of a "motivic" entity within it like a set-form expressed in the foreground.
2. The correlation between an arbitrarily or contextually selected temporal modulus and the pitch octave is dropped, and there is no temporal modular interval at all in this method.

Why no modulus? Because on the scale of division we are now considering, it seems perceptually impossible to sense the function of such an interval. It is one thing to consider a brief foreground measure expressed through this function, quite another to try one several tens or hundreds of beats long. Moreover, the abandonment of the modulus for time suggests the recognition of a fundamental difference between the musical dimensions of time and pitch: The pitch continuum is effectively finite (limited by what our ears can hear) and changes of direction within it are possible (it is a territory small enough to be spanned by a few modular intervals—eight or nine octaves altogether); in contrast, the temporal continuum is virtually infinite (limited only by how long we can stay awake), and one-directional only.

Here follows the set for a composition, first as a pitch-class ordering, then interpreted as a large-scale durational interval succession:

EXAMPLE 104

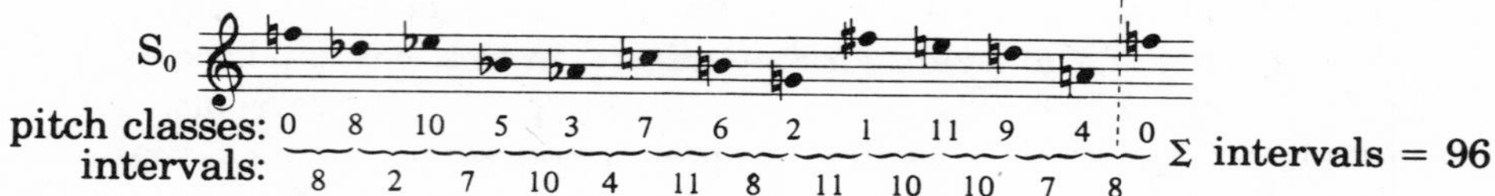

A one-unit interval ~ 10 ♩'s. Hence, total length = 10 x 96 = 960 ♩'s

Notice that the sizes of the durational intervals between the time points that correspond to the pitch classes of the set are scaled in accordance with a decision, made in advance, about how long the work is going to be. Here, we have decided that it will be 960 quarter-note beats at MM. 60—that is, 16 minutes. The sum of the intervals (*not* successive pitch-class numbers) is 96. This means that in terms of pitch class, the set spans 96 semitones from its origin and back. In durational terms, it means that it will span 96 time units. Units of what size? Having settled on 960 beats as a length, we can easily see that our set will divide this time span into 96 parts of 10 quarter-note beats each, since $960 = 10 \times 96$. Now if we take the interval succession as written under the set of example 104 (8 2 7 10 4 etc.), and translate its constituent intervals into temporal terms, in which ten beats corresponds to one semitone, we will generate a series of large sections, respectively of 10×8, 10×2, 10×7, etc., beats—that is: 960 quarter-note beats $= 80 + 20 + 70 + 100 + 40 + 110 + 80 + 110 + 100 + 100 + 70 + 80$ quarter-note beats, which added together will constitute the entire length of the piece.

What does all this tell us? So far, we have decided on a length for the work, and have now divided it into twelve sections. (We do this despite the fact that a starting point and eleven intervals are sufficient to define a 12-tone set; an eleven-interval division is perfectly reasonable, but the choice of twelve—the extra interval being that between the final and initial elements of the set—is suggested by traditional notions of closure and musical return, as well as by the arithmetic convenience that results from the fact that the sum of the twelve intervals thus defined is always an integral multiple of 12.) We have now made a first step of refinement and concretization: In an undifferentiated time continuum we have established twelve major sectional divisions. Let us now repeat the process, dividing each of our twelve sections internally into twelve intervals, again corresponding to those of the set. (The symbol ♩ here stands for "quarter-note beat"):

Section 1: 80 ♩'s. Sum of intervals = 96; therefore in temporal terms, an interval of size 1 in this section corresponds to $80/96$, or $5/6$ of a quarter-note beat. Therefore, the internal divisions of section 1 are $5/6 \times 8$, $5/6 \times 2$, etc., which yields the following succession of lengths, again given in beats:

$6\frac{2}{3}$, $1\frac{2}{3}$, $5\frac{5}{6}$, $8\frac{1}{3}$, $3\frac{1}{3}$, $9\frac{1}{6}$, $6\frac{2}{3}$, $9\frac{1}{6}$, $8\frac{1}{3}$,
$8\frac{1}{3}$, $5\frac{5}{6}$, $6\frac{2}{3}$; which adds up to 80 ♩.

Section 2: 20 ♩'s. An interval of size 1 here corresponds to $20/96 = 5/24$ of a quarter-note beat.

Therefore, the internal divisions, arrived at in the same way as for section 1, are (again in beats):

$1\frac{2}{3}$, $5/12$, $1\frac{11}{24}$, $2\frac{1}{12}$, $5/6$, $2\frac{7}{24}$, $1\frac{2}{3}$, $2\frac{7}{24}$, $2\frac{1}{12}$, $2\frac{1}{12}$,
$1\frac{11}{24}$, $1\frac{2}{3}$; which adds up to 20 ♩.

EXERCISE Calculate the internal divisions of each of the remaining sections 3 through 12, following the procedure given above.

Notice that because the set we are using contains intervals that are repeated, section lengths (at both levels we have so far reached—the larger section and its internal divisions) will likewise be repeated. In any case, we have refined and concretized matters yet a little more: After completing the exercise above, we now have 12 principal and 144 smaller sections. What they might eventually signify will emerge further on.

Let us now repeat the process of division on a third, and final, level of detail, dividing each of the 144 subsections as we have done with the larger sections into S-interval-proportional time intervals. Once again, because of the lengthiness of the process, we will only carry out the first few subdivisions.

For this third level, the division process will become unduly complex arithmetically unless we begin to round off some of the previously figured subsection lengths to integral numbers of beats, or simple fractions of them. In this spirit, we will adjust the internal lengths for section 1, preserving identities among the intervals and keeping to their approximate relative magnitudes:

Section 1: 80 ♩'s = 7, 2, 6, 8, 3, 9, 7, 9, 8, 8, 6, 7

We may express these as a series of different-sized measures, if we like, by using meter signatures:

$\begin{matrix} 7 & 2 & 6 & 8 \\ 4 & 4 & 4 & 4 \end{matrix}$ etc.

inside of each of which will be nested our third twelve-part division, according to the original interval succession. Thus we will divide the first $\frac{7}{4}$ into 80 equal parts, each of which equals 7/80 of a beat (which will now be our interval of size 1); and using this rather peculiar quantity, we will establish *approximate* lengths for the time intervals. At this level of detail, we may as well notate our results as a "rhythm," always remembering that it represents durational intervals, and not durations. Verification that our division is a fair approximation of the original interval succession is left to the reader:

EXAMPLE 105–a

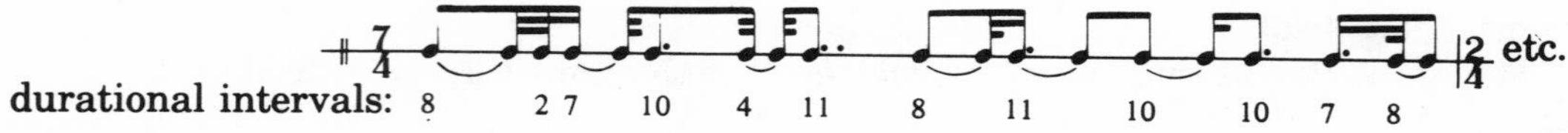

The $\frac{2}{4}$ that follows is so small that we may be best off giving up and just filling it with twelve equal divisions:

EXAMPLE 105–b

The following $\frac{6}{4}$ will have intervals a little smaller than those of the $\frac{7}{4}$, if we content ourselves with approximations:

EXAMPLE 105–c

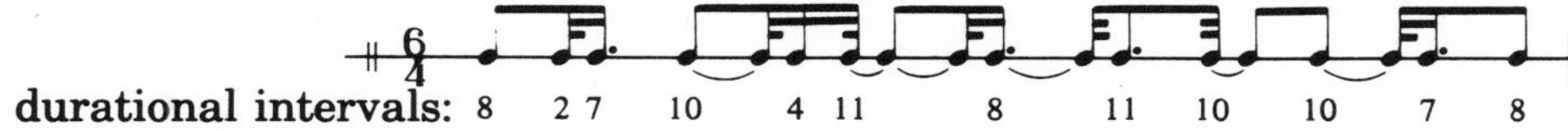

Notice that the beat subdivisions are chosen with regard to arithmetic convenience. But once they are decided, their selection will of course have a major effect on all subsequent stages of the compositional process. Here, in the case of our deriving the $\frac{6}{4}$ divisions from the $\frac{7}{4}$, note that one thirty-second note has been shaved from each durational interval, except for the four smallest intervals (2, 7, 4, 7), which have not been altered. In this way, all identities of length have been preserved in spite of our arithmetic adjustments.

You will have noticed that some of the durational intervals at our third level are extremely short, in the range of single or even fractional beats. In other words, whereas the largest intervals (at the first level of division) are of a size that suggests a role for them as major sectional divisions, and the second-level intervals nested in these largest divisions are of lengths generally appropriate for their serving as phrase-definers, the third-level intervals cannot be regarded as "sections" at all but rather as determinants of the location of specific musical events—most obviously, the attacks of notes. This is why we have notated our examples of the first-level divisions as quantities of beats, the second level as "measures" with "meter signatures," and the third as "rhythms."

This scheme of things begins to show a fundamental connection between foreground "rhythm" and background "form." Here we are proposing a specific method for compositional use that correlates them in a precisely defined way. But that does not alter the fact that in *all* music some correlation of these dimensions is at work, whether it has been consciously decided on or not. It should be clear that in using the term *form,* we are really only referring to a matter of scale or size. The crucial point is that rhythm and form are not different things but rather only the same basic thing expressed on different scales of size. Let us then, on this basis, eliminate once and for all the false distinction between "content" and "form"—as if there were a mystic elixir of artistic *content* which, if one could get hold of it, one would pour into bins of different shapes and sizes to produce different *forms*. "Content" might then be redefined as small-scale form, "form" as large-scale content.

And once again we must emphasize that the large sectional divisions, and their smaller internally nested intervals of time, do *not* represent durations. They denote the locations of time points, whose meanings have yet to be determined. It is most likely that the smallest divisions will be regarded as marking the starting points of tones, but—for example—the notated durations in our third-level examples do not indicate or imply that the arrival of one time point terminates what the preceding time point had initiated. Thus, if we attach a succession of set-derived notes to the time points of example 105-c, we might express them as a tune:

EXAMPLE 106–a

as an arpeggiation of chords:

EXAMPLE 106–b

as several chords repeated:

EXAMPLE 106–c

as partitioned into counterpoint, here in three voices:

EXAMPLE 106-d

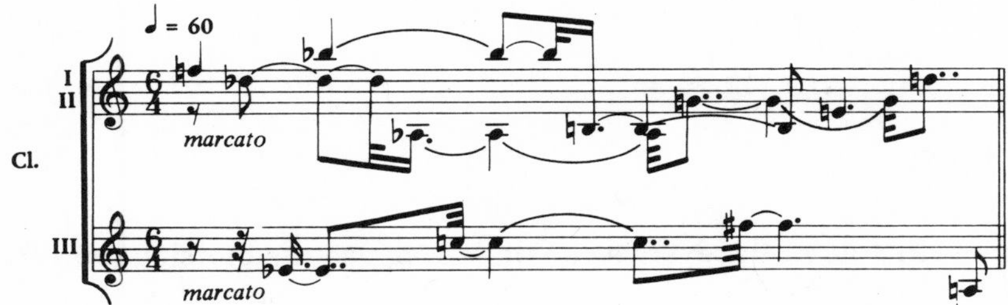

or as an infinite number of other things, whatever may be useful and apposite in the composition under construction.

EXERCISE Consider the set 0 5 1 3 4 2 7 9 11 8 6 10 and the time length 300 ♩ 's at ♩ = 72.
Span this total length with the intervals of the set, writing out the first-, then the second-, and finally the third-level sectional divisions, using the procedures presented in the text. Make an array for the set, and choose set-forms so that you attach one pitch class to each of the time points resulting from the process of successive sectional divisions. Now articulate this time-point/pitch-class succession into a piece for piano.
(N.B. For very short intervals at the third level, use grace notes and gather attacks that are extremely close together into chords.)

So far, we have dealt only with a "single-line division" of large spans of musical time. But just as smaller-scale time-point sets can be combined in various ways "contrapuntally," so can these larger complexes of time division be combined "polyphonically." A work might then consist of the simultaneous unfolding of several complexes of time division similar to the ones outlined above. (An explanation of how this can be accomplished is the subject of the second part of this chapter.)

Other general points remain to be made, however. When we contemplate the structures we have now created, it begins to appear that adherence to generation of them by 12-tone sets is not really a *sine qua non,* especially if issues of combinatoriality are set aside. What now emerges is that *ordered interval successions* are the real determinants: The fact that they happen to define 12-tone sets is less significant. This is not to suggest the abandonment of such conventional and richly fruited constructs; there is no reason not to continue using the 12-tone system in all its harmonic resources. But it does suggest that many different kinds of music might be made using ordered interval successions as the basis of their forms and pitch-class structures with less than or more than twelve elements; and therefore that repetition of elements is also a possibility.

EXERCISES

A. Proceeding as in the exercise on page 155, use the division process we have outlined above to generate a piece from the ordered succession given in each case:

1. Starting with the following hexachord, use a span of 140 beats, and only employ the inner five intervals:

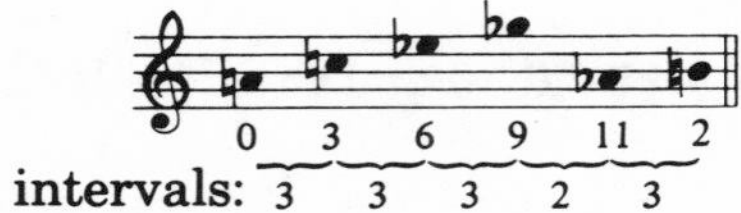

2. For the following 24-element set, use a span of 324 beats, employing only the inner 23 intervals; make the division on two levels only:

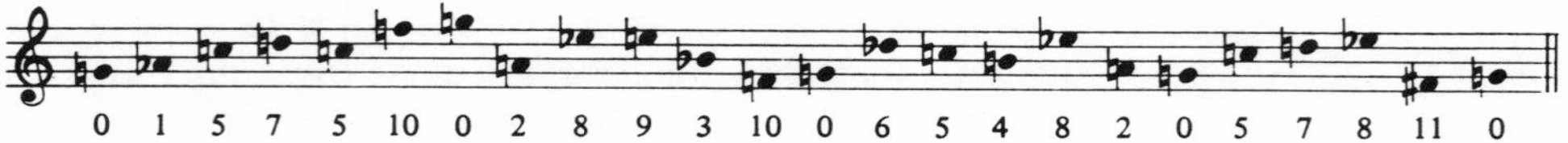

3. For the following permutation of the diatonic pitch-class collection (i.e., the major scale), use 240 beats:

B. After you have completed the division process for all three exercises above, attach pitch-class successions derived from the basic sets involved; choose your own instrumentation.

The Nesting Method

In the first section of this chapter, we presented the large-to-small, or "outside-to-inside," application of the principles of the time-point system. Let us reiterate the basic procedure we followed. We began with the largest dimension—the total duration of the composition, as projected in our initial planning. This total duration we then divided up into time intervals proportional to and in the same order as those of the pitch-class set we had selected for the work—thus retaining the time-point system's principle of correlating pitch interval with time interval; but we noted the important difference of abandoning the notion of a temporal modulus. Then we repeated the division process twice more, and achieved a highly detailed division for the flow of time in our piece, so detailed that we would be entitled to regard the finest divisions as foreground rhythm. Then we decided on what to attach to the time points which these manifoldly nested interval successions had located for us—usually pitch classes, generated according to some reasonable successional scheme from the composition's pitch-class set and its derivatives.

At this point, we really have all we need for a piece, provided that we continue the essential task of turning pitch classes into notes (by giving registral, etc., values to them), and fields of notes into lines and simultaneities: in other words, carving melody out of the array of relations. However, as we mentioned above, near the end of this chapter's first section, the time-point system can be contrapuntally extended to control the large form of a work. But before considering these polyphonic extensions of the basic method, the reader is advised to refer back to chapter 4 to review some of the ways in which arrays of pitch-class/time-point relationships should be transformed into music.

Now to begin. Counterpoint, although it may be successfully partitioned out of a single large spanning with its associated interior nestings of intervals, can also have a fruitful polyphonic basis at a more fundamental level, as we have remarked. This is achieved by the simultaneous spanning of the single piece-length by more than one interval succession. In the following outline, the total length of the work to be composed is spanned simultaneously by the interval succession of S and its associated R:

S: 0 5 4 1 11 9 2 10 8 3 6 7 0
intervals: 5 11 9 10 10 5 8 10 7 3 1 5 = Sum of intervals = 84

R: 0 7 6 3 8 10 2 9 11 1 4 5 0
intervals: 7 11 9 5 2 4 7 2 2 3 1 7 = Sum of intervals = 60

If the time length = 420 ♩ 's, then an interval of size 1 in S is equivalent to 5 ♩ 's, and an interval of size 1 in R is equivalent to 7 ♩ 's.

The two strands of division, based respectively on the intervals of S and R and reconciled so that the different intervallic sums for the two forms will both occupy the same time length, may be tabulated thus (in quarter-note beats):

S	25	55	45	50	50	25	40	50	35	15	5	25
R	49	77	63	35	14	28	49	14	14	21	7	49

Again notice that the sum of intervals of each of the two forms is different—84 and 60, respectively—and that since they are both spanning the same total number of beats, the correlation between intervals of pitch and durational intervals is different in the two cases: For S, a one-unit interval corresponds to 5 beats; for R, 7 beats. Naturally, a similar situation will persist when the division process is carried out on more local levels. And here, let us parenthetically note that if the sum of intervals (always including a twelfth interval, from the last element to the first) of a set is:

12, then the sums for its R or its I will be 132
24, then the sums for its R or its I will be 120
36, then the sums for its R or its I will be 108
48, then the sums for its R or its I will be 96
60, then the sums for its R or its I will be 84
72, then the sums for its R or its I will be 72

and conversely. Note also that the sums of intervals for S and RI are always the same.

The polyphonic structure we have begun to sketch can be for any desired number of voices, but two, three, or four seems the most practical, since each voice at this level is not so much a "line" as it is the potential generator of elaborate surface detail. Here is an example of a four-voice model, first singly divided and then extended to the second level of division. We make use of the set used already for S and R divisions, now adding RI and I as well. In both the larger and smaller divisions, we show only the start of the process, as its full extent is too lengthy:

Elapsed ♩'s:	25	80	125	175	225	250				
Voice 1: **S**	25	55	45	50	50	25	40			
Voice 2: **RI**	25	5	15	35	50	40	25	50	50	etc.
Voice 3: **R**	49	77	63	35	14					
Voice 4: **I**	49	7	21	14	14	49	28	14	35	63
Elapsed ♩'s:	49	56	77	91	105	154	182	196	231	

Remember that the interval succession of RI is the reverse of that for S; and that of I is the reverse of that for R.

EXERCISE Complete the above diagram to determine the larger section-lengths, reading the applicable intervals from the enumeration on page 158. Be sure to align the sections in each voice correctly with respect to those of the other voices; I recommend keeping for each voice a running total of the sum of section lengths (in beats) for this purpose.

Here follows the beginning of the second level of division for the above diagram of larger section lengths. The second-level divisions are expressed as meter signatures. In our illustration, we are using the RI interval succession to divide the larger sections in the S-voice; the S-intervals for the RI voice; and correspondingly for the R and I voices.

Voice	Section	Meter signatures
S	25 ♩'s	1½/4, ¼/4, ⅞/4, 2/4, 3/4, 2⅜/4, 1½/4, 3/4, 3/4, 2¾/4, 3¼/4, 1½/4
S	55♩'s	
RI	25 ♩'s	1½/4, 3¼/4, 2¾/4, 3/4, 3/4, 1½/4, 2⅜/4, 3/4, 2/4, ⅞/4, ¼/4, 1½/4
RI	5 ♩'s	
R	49 ♩'s	5¾/4, ⅞/4, 2½/4, 1⅝/4, 1⅝/4, 5¾/4, 3¼/4, 1⅝/4
I	49 ♩'s	5¾/4, 9/4, 7⅜/4, 4/4

etc.

(The meter signatures above are all expressed in terms of a quarter-note beat; hence the fractional numerators.)

In this example there are not only four different forms of the basic interval succession determining the largest-scale divisions, but also internally in each polyphonic voice other forms are used to divide up the larger durational intervals. It cannot be stressed too strongly that an infinite number of such combinations of forms exists and can yield good results. Notice also that, just as previously, we have not hesitated to make arithmetic adjustments of the results of the small-scale divisions; the correlation between pitch-class interval size and durational interval size is therefore sometimes only approximate. This procedure is adopted for convenience, but it is not the result of mere caprice; for time lengths are not nearly so exactly perceived as are pitch intervals, and a degree of exactitude involving small fractions of beats serves no purpose beyond needless complication. In making adjustments of this kind, try to preserve identities wherever they existed in the original interval succession, and as much as possible, preserve simple length-proportional relations—so that, for instance, an interval twice the size of another retains this relation after adjustment. This we recommend because simple length proportions like 2:1 are perceived rather precisely.

Now let us turn to subsidiary devices for beginning the process of articulating the time-point/pitch-class structures produced by our method into something musically concrete. Take the following excerpt from such a structure:

EXAMPLE 107

(Here the durational intervals are from S; the pitch classes from, S_0 followed by R_0.)

In its present form, this excerpt already embodies an important device—a simple density relation between time points and pitch classes. There is not just one pitch class per time point but a variable number, running through the sequence 1, 2, 3, 1, 2, 3, . . . Thus some time points become the initiation points of simultaneities, whether expressed as actual chords, contrapuntal components, or as content groups for free "arpeggiation" within the confines of the durational interval that the time point and its successor time points define. This last possibility is particularly appropriate for long durational intervals. Furthermore, the density-relation scheme here is a simple cyclically increasing one. It would be easy, if one wanted to, to extract a more elaborate scheme from the set itself—say, one directly proportional to the succession of interval sizes. In finding ways of correlating the pitch-class content of the work with the formal/rhythmic designs we have been discussing, one may make the operations and relations as complex as one chooses; but bear in mind that the place for complexities and ornate detail, if it exists at all, is in the *surface* of the piece. If one makes the underlying structure overly elaborate, its various interior interrelations will tend to cancel each other's effectiveness. That is why we usually prefer simpler schemes.

Now let us turn to register. Considering example 107, we could give its constituent lines registral values directly according to the general melodic principles we described in chapter 4. But we might also first want to make register a general function, operative over large regions of the piece, just as we have with time-point/pitch-class correlation. In doing this, I suggest that the registral areas involved be only generally defined—high, middle, and low, for example, or perhaps a comparable four-part division. The reason for this lies in the necessity not to pre-define register so narrowly that the application of a general registral scheme will unduly constrain the placement of individual notes at whatever octave is required by other demands of the piece. When it does, it is very difficult to follow the essential melodic principles which alone are capable of creating pleasing melody. So, again as in the case of pitch classes and time points, let the scheme of registral alternations and combinations be simple. We might, for example, assign to the successive smaller-scale subdivisions whose beginnings were sketched on page 159, a scheme of registral alternation for each voice, defined as follows:

1. Take the interval succession of S *mod* 3. This will give three distinct values (0, 1, 2).
2. Interpret these three values as referring to three registral regions—low, middle, high.
3. Locate the pitch content of each smaller-scale subdivision by assigning one of these S-derived registral values to each successive subdivision.

Carrying out this scheme is left to the reader.

After all this is done, we will have translated the pitch-class content of our structure into real notes, applying melodic principles to give them their final roles in actual lines.

Now we have a piece of articulated counterpoint. It could stand as is, but there is no reason why each new attack in a line need displace the note sounding before it, or why a uniform "legato," as implied in what we have produced so far, need be the only possibility. Say, for instance, that we adopt the following articulation sequence: arpeggiation, with the elements all sustained; overlapping of notes in pairs; legato; semi-legato; staccato. We might apply each of these types of articulation to a few successive notes—the number either being constant, or given by a device similar to the one we presented for density of pitch classes. If such a simple sostenuto-to-staccato scheme is applied separately but simultaneously in our four voices, what was previously a legato single-line combination becomes a richly varied complex, some of it *secco,* some arpeggiated, and some in between.

In dealing with these transformations we have been discussing a number of possibilities simultaneously. We must again emphasize that these are all merely samples of a method of working, an attitude toward the compositional process. An enormous number of other reasonable possibilities also exist, and we have presented only a few, to serve as a guide.

One last remark: All of our time divisions have been given in terms of beats rather than absolute time lengths, though they too would be perfectly workable. Our reason for doing this is that musical time passes not through the hearer's recognition of absolute time lengths but through his perception of a series of events. If, for instance, a series of beats is articulated, we are still likely to consider it and receive it as a succession of equally stressed events, even though it may accelerate or retard. Musical time is a "qualitative" flow, made so through quantitative means. Expressing our fundamental time relations in beats reflects this fundamental property. It leaves us free, without violating the basic proportional schemes we have developed for our work, to vary the size of the beat, to vary the tempo, for expressive and inflectional purposes. It makes our work flexible.

Valedictory

In the last chapter we described methods for producing the large shape of pieces. What this really means is that we have sought devices that can integrate our fairly clear intuitive perception of what is an appropriate way to express pitch-class relations already established in the small dimension with a sense of what an appropriate large shape for such moment-to-moment relations might be. But—and particularly after a certain amount of experience—is it not also possible to make such large shapes directly, by intuitive and contextual response to the pitch-class arrays themselves? Certainly it is, but the beginner might be well advised not to assume that such a skill is inborn, just because it is non-verbal. He will need some years of discipline in more fully rationalized methods before he attempts to scale these heights. Nevertheless, just as the rhythmic, and therefore the large-scale structural, functions of tonal music developed gradually out of many composers' responses to the new pitch-relational premises introduced by the system, so the same process is no doubt going on in the newer world of chromatic pitch relations. And an individual composer, too, may reproduce in himself these larger historical processes.

In doing so, the common ground between diatonic and chromatic music, the underlying concerns that produce both, may become clear. It certainly begins to seem that, as we observed at the beginning of this book, the two domains are not exclusive, but rather form parts of a continuous whole. If the highly chromatic music of late tonality can be regarded as proto-12-tone; if the last, 12-tone, works of Stravinsky can contain so many tonal-system puns—then surely our awareness of the two approaches to composition as parts of a single generous totality must become vivid indeed.

The question of "rigor" is often raised these days, and my suggestions that rationalized methods of composition may be succeeded by more "direct" ones no doubt may lead to invoking it here as well. But I believe that no compositional method can be "proved" to be worth anything in particular; it can only be shown to produce pieces which, subjectively, are considered worthwhile. There is therefore nothing but practical value in compositional method. No virtue inheres *a priori* in any specific procedure for composing. But all the methods and principles outlined in this book are based on many years of experience by many different composers. If their work is judged of value, then the methods may be so judged as well. And, to quote from the preface to a text in another field by Richard Courant: "To me it seems extremely important that the student should be warned from the very beginning against a smug and presumptuous purism; this is not the least of my purposes in writing this book."

However this may be, the obverse of the coin of methodological fetishism is the detestable anti-intellectualism of the present age. Let us instead propose an attempt to become cultivated: to understand the necessary balance between the dictates of reason (that is, slowed-down intuition) and the role of intuition in all human creation—particularly in the arts, where each work created is a universe of itself.

Finally, I would caution the beginning composer against resisting the necessary and healthful discipline that must always precede the acquisition of real skill and understanding. It seems to me a universal in all times and places that art requires for its highest practice a long initial period of subjecting the self and submitting to constraint and discipline. Then, after some decades in this condition, an artist may truly discard all method, "learn to unlearn his learning," and function fully in the direct interplay between his own intuition and the nature of the world at large. These remarks seem to me necessary to counter the frequently advocated pablum of "self-expression" which so often in this age misguides the young. This seductive notion of self-expression, merchandized to those who have as yet no self to express, is the most dangerous and destructive idea to corrupt a young composer. Remember always that freedom can be had only if it is earned; in art it is earned by prior submission to discipline. And remember too that freedom means nothing unless there are co-ordinates, fixed and clear, whose very immobility allows the one who is free to measure the unfetteredness of his flight.

Selected Bibliography

BABBITT, MILTON. "Set Structure as a Compositional Determinate." *Journal of Music Theory* 5, No. 1 (1961): 72–94. Reprinted in *Perspectives on Contemporary Music Theory*, eds. Benjamin Boretz and Edwin Cone, pp. 129–47. New York: W. W. Norton & Co., Inc., 1972.

——. "Some Aspects of Twelve-Tone Composition." *The Score and I.M.A. Magazine* (June 1955): 53–61. Reprinted in *Twentieth Century Views of Music History* (with Addenda by Gerald Warfield), pp. 364–71. New York: Charles Scribner's Sons, Inc., 1972.

——. "Twelve-Tone Invariants as Compositional Determinates." *The Musical Quarterly* 46 (1960): 246–59. Entire volume reprinted as *Problems of Modern Music*. New York: W. W. Norton & Co., Inc., 1960.

——. "Twelve-Tone Rhythmic Structure and the Electronic Medium." *Perspectives of New Music* 1, No. 1 (1962): 49–79. Reprinted in *Perspectives on Contemporary Music Theory,* eds. Benjamin Boretz and Edwin Cone, pp. 148–79. New York: W. W. Norton & Co., Inc., 1972.

FORTE, ALLEN. *The Structure of Atonal Music*. New Haven: Yale University Press, 1973.

MARTINO, DONALD. "The Source Set and its Aggregate Formations." *Journal of Music Theory* 5, No. 2 (1961): 224–73.

PERLE, GEORGE. *Serial Composition and Atonality*, 4th ed. Berkeley: University of California Press, 1977.

RAHN, JOHN. *Basic Atonal Theory.* New York: Longman Inc., 1979. (forthcoming)

STARR, DANIEL and MORRIS, ROBERT. "A General Theory of Combinatoriality and the Aggregate (Part I)." *Perspectives of New Music* 16, No. 1 (1977): 3–35.

WESTERGAARD, PETER. "Toward a Twelve-Tone Polyphony." *Perspectives of New Music* 4, No. 2 (1966): 90–112. Reprinted in *Perspectives on Contemporary Music Theory*, eds. Benjamin Boretz and Edwin Cone, pp. 238–60. New York: W. W. Norton & Co., Inc., 1972.

Index